Our Spiritual Evolution

Transcending the Third Dimension

Mark Gilbert

Conscious
Bridge
Publishing

Our Spiritual Evolution:
Transcending the Third Dimension
Copyright © 2014 by Mark Gilbert
All rights reserved.

Publisher: Conscious Bridge Publishing
ISBN: 978-0-9883032-1-8
Book and Cover Design: Gary D. Hall,
    Greystroke Creative
Editorial Services: Alexi Paulina

Printed in the United States of America
Copies of this book may be ordered from:
www.amazon.com
http://consciousbridge.com

*To Mary, for all her support
in my own spiritual evolution.*

Other Books by Mark Gilbert

Be Yourself: Evolving the World Through Personal Empowerment

Our Spiritual Rights and Responsibilities

Becoming a Spiritual Change Agent

Table of Contents

Introduction

You and I are on a journey. Everyone is. We are on a spiritual, evolutionary journey. This book is about understanding that journey, how it plays a role in your life, and the role you play in its direction.

Each of us was born into our individual lives here on Earth. We have moved through a timeline of experiences from birth up to this moment. Along the way we have tried to make sense of these experiences – to give them some meaning. Understanding life's meaning is what this book is about.

Those experiences have played out in two realms. First, there is the physical aspect of our lives. Second, there are those experiences that seem to transcend our physical nature. We are material animals, while simultaneously we are spiritual beings. This book is intended to help you understand that dichotomy.

There is no denying that we experience the world of matter. We have material bodies that appear to be the product of eons of physical evolution. We have an animalistic nature. We are motivated by physical needs for air, water, food, and more. We desire affection, bodily touch, sex, and sensory stimulation.

Our senses present to us a world that appears to be "out there." This world overwhelmingly demands our attention. For many people, the material world is the only world. This material world is what I refer to as "the third dimension." Yes, as we move through the timeline of our life, much of our experience is defined by the world of objects and their interactions – in other words, by our relationship with the third dimension.

The second way we are experience our lives is through an inner, subjective realm that cannot be denied. We know it through our thoughts, and through our consciousness. Somewhere we link our consciousness to our bodies. This physical "thing" that we call "our body" appears to carry around some nonphysical thing that we know as our subjective experience.

Contained within our consciousness – our subjective nature – is a mixture of our sensory awareness of the current moment, our memories of this lifetime, our hopes and dreams for our future, our beliefs and worldviews, and our access to wisdom through something we label as *intuition*. We are motivated by nonmaterial needs: love, self-esteem, a desire to do our best, a call to make a difference in the world, and more. We desire to transcend these material bodies and connect with something greater and more expansive than our individual lives. In other words, we have a spiritual nature.

As we navigate through these two realms of the experiences that we label "our life," we can't help but ask ourselves questions such as why are we here, why do we exist, and is there meaning to life? Most of us have pondered these concerns at some point. It is these questions that we will touch on in this book.

It is these deeper questions that have long motivated me. I remember being a young boy, lying outside in the grass and staring at the sky, wondering what was up there. Yes, there were clouds, the sun, the moon, and the stars. But why were they there? And why was I here on this ground, looking up at them? I'd heard stories about a place called heaven and an old man called God. Were they up there too?

For the most part, I kept these questions to myself. No one else seemed to be asking them, and I wondered if something might be wrong with me for having these thoughts. I remember being taken to church and Sunday school as a child, but even there I didn't hear anything that helped me understand why I existed. In fact, I could not comprehend why people went to church. The teachings presented held no relevance for me. At best, they were boring. At worst, they appeared to serve only the need to make me feel guilty about being human. That didn't seem right.

When I started college, I was asked to declare a major, and I picked psychology. My motivation at the time was that I was hoping that psychology would answer these deeper questions of meaning. Unfortunately, the brand of psychology being taught at the time – *behavioralism* – did not delve into such deeper issues. Only occasionally, in brief snippets, did we touch on such topics as what motivates humans or the question of consciousness.

As I grew into an adult, much of my focus was directed toward my family and career. I had to make a living here on planet Earth, and to provide for my wife and children. There was little time left over to spend on deeper issues. But somehow, I did find time to read about Eastern religions, New Age beliefs, metaphysical concepts, and meditation. I practiced meditation with the intent that I would get into some altered state of consciousness and life's meaning would be revealed to me finally. No such experience happened—at least not in the manner that I was expecting.

I read about the mind-altering effects of drugs and wondered if they held the key that I sought. I never tried them, so I can't answer that question. Why? Maybe it was fear. Maybe it was my overwhelming personal sense of responsibility in being a father, husband, and provider. In addition, I just didn't travel in circles where drugs were available.

But I did keep searching—visiting metaphysical bookstores, reading books on consciousness and spirituality, and continuing to meditate off and on. I even went to churches on occasion. Eventually I found a philosophy called Science of Mind, which was developed by a man named Ernest Holmes. Holmes studied science, philosophy, and religion, and synthesized the threads of truth he found in all of them into his practical philosophy which he began teaching in the early 20th century.

I took classes where I studied the Science of Mind and then began applying it to my life. I can honestly say that this philosophy changed my life for the better. However, it wasn't all just intellectual study. Over time I developed a routine and regular schedule of meditation. I let go of my previous expectations concerning a specific experience that I expected to occur. Releasing my preconceived ideas of what I was supposed to "get" from meditation opened me to the space of truly receiving its gifts. Although it is hard to describe these gifts in words, I'll give it a try.

By quieting my mind and just allowing myself to sit and be in the moment, I began developing an experientially based appreciation for the oneness of life. This didn't happen overnight. It certainly didn't happen in some flash of insight, like I had been hoping for. Instead, it was more like a slow and steady development over time, much like building muscles through exercise. My meditation practice built my "spiritual muscles." As this occurred, I found myself releasing my attachments to small, petty things that had concerned me before, and being more open to forgiving others when they did not act as I desired. I felt myself opening my heart to caring about more and more people, and beginning to live from the space where I realized that everything was connected.

In the midst of all of this, something else started happening. As I meditated, ideas would flood into my awareness. At first I tried to block them, thinking it was just my "monkey mind" trying to distract me from a good meditation experience. However, something in my intuition finally convinced me to listen to these ideas. I began to see them less as distractions and more as a divine flow of information moving through me. I began to see the gift I was being given. I started a practice of journaling after such meditations, so as to capture the ideas coming through me.

I eventually went on to become a spiritual counselor and minister with the philosophy of Science of Mind. I currently work for the organization whose mission is to bring this philosophy to the world. However, even though the Science of Mind is woven through this book, this book is not simply about it.

Instead, this book offers a viewpoint on life drawn and synthesized from numerous sources where I have found truth. In addition to Holmes, I have found great worth in understanding life through the study of Abraham Maslow, Clare Graves and Spiral Dynamics, Ken Wilber and Integral Theory, and others. My continuous reading, study, and synthesis, coupled with the ideas that were coming through my meditations, led to my publishing a blog site called Conscious Bridge (www.consciousbridge.com). There, since January 2010, I have been presenting my own views on these deeper questions. Many of the chapters in this book were originally published on Conscious Bridge. As I present this material again in book format, I have edited, reorganized, and updated the content.

The goal of Conscious Bridge has always been to present ideas that will help us on our journey—both the physical one and the spiritual one. I know deeply that we are all on an evolutionary journey moving through this worldly experience. It is my belief that evolution's trajectory is for us to realize that we are all one, that everything is connected, and that we came from and will return to the same source. The tagline for the website is "Evolving to Oneness."

The goal of this book is the same: to open your awareness to our oneness. That, however, is a fairly broad topic. To be more specific, this book is designed to be a highly accessible introduction to understanding our spiritual evolution—both our "involutionary" journey away from oneness and our "evolutionary" return to oneness. I trust you will begin looking at life through what I call an "evolutionary lens." You will start seeing evidence all around you that confirms that we are moving and growing through an evolutionary process—one that is more inclusive than is taught by neo-Darwinian science.

Ultimately, my hope is that as you read this book (and possibly the ideas presented on my website) that you receive some insights that help you to understand your experience of life and assist you along your spiritual journey.

Blessings and love,
Mark Gilbert

Chapter One

Overview of Our Evolutionary Journey

In this opening chapter, I will provide an overview of our evolutionary journey. This is the key foundation for the detail covered in the chapters that follow.

In this overview, I will use the time-tested method of *self-dialogue*. I will succinctly explore humanity's evolution through the third dimension, and our opportunity to transcend it. Such self-dialogues have long been used by philosophers, from the *Dialogues of Plato* to Ken Wilber's *A Brief History of Everything*. As you read the conversation, consider this to be a dialogue—the bold text representing your "questioning self," and the regular text representing the response from your "answering self" (or what you might consider your "higher self"). Let's get started!

First of all, as this book is about "transcending the third dimension," maybe we should start by describing what you mean when you say *third dimension?*

The third dimension is this physical reality in which we find ourselves living. The sense that I am right here and you are over there, that I am separate and apart from everything *else, and t*hat I am moving through all this other stuff in a linear experience of time (time is generally considered to be a "fourth dimension")—are all aspects of our third-dimensional experience. All the physical matter and energy that we experience in a world of space and time, where everything has a distinct location in a distinct moment, is an aspect of the third dimension. Mathematically speaking, the first dimension is a point, the second dimension is a flat plane (much like a sheet of paper), and the third dimension is where we experience depth. In this book, I use the term *third dimension* to reference our personal and collective experience on this material plane.

Why does the third dimension exist?

In my view, it exists as a sort of school or playground where growth and experiences can occur. It's a place where Spirit or ultimate oneness can allow aspects of itself to divide and sense themselves as being separate and apart from one another—and have experiences of such separation. It's a place that we move through on our way back to oneness and unity.

How did we get here?

That question can be answered in a couple of ways. As many mystics and sages have pointed out, if God (or Spirit, or oneness, or infinite intelligence, or whatever name you wish to give ultimate reality) knows and senses everything that ever is or ever was or ever will be, all in the one instant of the holy moment, then what experience remains that is unknown? Their answer was that infinite intelligence was called to divide itself, not in reality but only in aspects of its awareness. It placed "parts" of itself in compartmentalized pockets that considered themselves separate from the other compartmentalized pockets. Each considered itself separate from the others. The end result was something often called "multiplicity within the unity": the sense of multiple things that are ultimately united in one. These compartmentalized pieces of Spirit were thrown into the third dimension so that Spirit could have the experience of separation and all that comes with that: relationships with other separate things, and the free will to choose one thing over another.

Traditional religion often refers to this process as "the fall": We lived in perfection in oneness, but fell into the world of duality, the world of good and bad, and right and wrong. And, it took those individual experiences of separation and divided them into distinct "moments in time" (again, technically a fourth dimension) that we experience in a linear fashion. Ultimately, each of us has this experience of being separate and apart from everything else and moving through a sequence of such experiences. Through this process, ultimate Spirit gets to break up our sense of unity—both in space and time—into a sense of distinct units. So, one way of explaining why we are here is that it allows Spirit or God to have this experience.

Then what is the other way you can describe we came to be here?

This is where science comes in—it describes our third-dimensional origin as being from "the Big Bang." Although science is, for the most part, silent about what preceded this beginning moment, current scientific thinking is that all physical matter was contained in a very hot, very dense area that exploded outward very quickly. At the moment of this expansion, all the physical laws that we have since "discovered" already existed. One such law was gravity, which acted upon the unevenness in this soupy plasma to begin bringing matter together into very hot and dense stars containing hydrogen and helium. Through a process of collapse and expansion caused by gravity, stars went through a lifecycle that ultimately created the other elements and cast them out into space. Through time, gravity brought together dense pockets of matter, such as planets that moved into gravitational orbits around other stars. Certain planets developed conditions favorable for third-dimensional life to evolve. The process of evolution also was embedded in everything from the moment of the Big Bang. This process favored life to build up in greater and greater degrees of complexity, from single-cell organisms to more complex organisms, and on up the chain to humanity.

So, how did life come from inert matter?

That's a magical question that science really doesn't answer. The common description is that physical conditions simply arose that were conducive for "life to emerge." One has to consider that the potential for this emergence always existed. This begs the question, how and why did that potential become embedded into this dimension?

How do these two stories, the fall from unity into multiplicity and our physical evolutionary path from the Big Bang, interrelate?

As I see it, Spirit's creation of the multiplicity for the experience it offered began with the creation of the third dimension via the Big Bang. Infinite intelligence created all matter and all laws (including gravity and evolution) in that first moment, embedding itself into everything. It has allowed these aspects of itself to evolve and to experience all that the evolutionary process entails. This evolutionary aspect of the third dimension not only allowed planets to form, but enabled life to emerge on the planets—and from life, and ultimately, consciousness emerged. Or, perhaps more correctly, we might say that ultimately *our awareness of consciousness emerged*.

What is consciousness, and how did it emerge?

That's another of those magical questions. The nature of consciousness has been a subject of interest for philosophers and scientists for a long time. Some even question whether its existence is truly real. The great irony, of course, is that such questioning is created within that person's consciousness. On some level, it is funny to hear scientists using their individual consciousness to deny that it exists! We humans experience consciousness as our self-awareness: the part of us that assimilates the combination of our sensory input, our thoughts, and our memories to create this persona or ego that we sense as ourselves. Stop for a moment and ask yourself, "Who am I?" Most likely the picture you come up with is a bundle that includes a physical body and a sense of its awareness of itself. That awareness is your experience of consciousness. You can only know your experience of it. You can't know my experience, although you can imagine that mine is similar to yours. Yet we can also imagine that some aspect of this consciousness is experienced by other animals as well. I know that my dog has consciousness of some type. Science tells us (when it chooses to discuss the subject at all) that consciousness "emerged" at some point in the evolutionary process. Where in the evolutionary chain consciousness first occurred is subject to debate. The reason for the existence of consciousness also is debated. Some scientists believe it is simply some meaningless byproduct of the physical evolution of our brains. Others point to the possibility that consciousness gives its owner an evolutionary advantage, so that it just naturally developed out of the "survival of the fittest." But again, one has to consider and wonder about the fact that the potential existed from the Big Bang onward for the emergence of consciousness.

From where do you think consciousness emerged?

I believe what some philosophers, mystics, and a few scientists have been saying: that consciousness was there all along. It is only our experience of it that has emerged. Consciousness is embedded in everything. It is in the smallest bits of matter and is in all energy. There is nothing that does not contain consciousness. Even subatomic particles and single-cell organisms have a degree of consciousness. What is it within them that gives them "agency," the ability to hold themselves as distinct entities and interact appropriately with the rest of the world? That "something" is the consciousness or intelligence embedded within them.

But wait, you're making consciousness sound like Spirit!

That's right. I believe Spirit is ultimately consciousness. The One Infinite Consciousness embedded its nature (consciousness) in everything. Consciousness is, as many say, "the ground of all Being." It is the connecting aspect of the universe that allows everything to be created and experienced. Consciousness is not a by-product of our brains, as many scientists seem to believe. Consciousness is the underlying field that gives rise to all matter, including our brains. That piece of us that experiences consciousness is our tasting the Oneness from which we sprang. The evolutionary process by which matter built up higher degrees of consciousness led to humanity crossing a threshold into self-awareness as part of its return to oneness. If we can imagine all of our little individual pockets of consciousness being reunited into a single awareness (a stretch for our minds, I agree), then we can get a sense of consciousness at the level of Spirit.

If this is our evolutionary past, then what's next for humanity?

That depends on whom you ask. Although science is a great tool for empirically testing how things work in the physical world, most scientists don't like to make predictions about the future. Sure, we can use science to look at past trends in certain areas and describe their likely future trajectory for specific areas of life. Consider for a moment the charts we've seen on carbon-dioxide emissions and their relationship to Earth's rising temperatures. Or, consider descriptions of how the pace of technological change will increase exponentially in the future. Although science allows us to make these limited projections, most scientists avoid trying to predict overall what the future may hold for humanity. Futurists, however, often meld the observable trends together to provide a broader description of our potential future. Some even delve into the realm of consciousness a bit, pointing to growing trends in body-mind medicine, altruism and spirituality, and then attempting to offer what might be on the horizon for us based upon these trends. This information is useful for glimpsing what might be coming next, but doesn't really touch on where humanity may ultimately be going. However, mystics and philosophers have described an end game where we return to our source. They say that we are headed toward higher and greater levels of awareness, where ultimately we live in oneness.

How can we continue our evolution and return to the unity from which we came? How do we transcend the third dimension?

There are several layers to the answers to these questions. First we must consider the role that each of us plays in our personal evolution. Each of us must ask ourselves, "What must I do to transcend the third dimension and evolve personally?" Second, there is the process in which humanity is collectively evolving—from individuals on their own path to a collective humanity evolving at a societal, worldwide level, as well as in our collective consciousness. We must consider, how is this communal process playing out, and what is our role in contributing to it? Furthermore, behind all this is a basic assumption that we wish to transcend the third dimension. Is this true? Are we called to move beyond here? Is there a "beyond here"? Humanity is certainly at an interesting point in its evolution.

Before we consider our personal or collective role in what may be coming next, and the evolutionary journey, maybe you should first describe what you mean when you say that ultimately "humanity will transcend the third dimension." What exactly does that mean?

In my thinking, it means that some aspect of us will move beyond the limitations created by living in a world of time and space, where things appear to be separate from one another. Although I certainly have no insider knowledge about the characteristics of life beyond the third dimension, I imagine that it entails leaving behind the need for a physical body as we know it, as well as moving beyond the experience of linear time. My belief is that the aspect of our being that we carry with us from the third dimension to wherever we go relates to our sense of self, our consciousness.

Is this transcendence done by each of us individually?

Good question! On a certain level, I believe it is. Each of us grows and evolves at an individual level that ultimately leads to our personal transcendence beyond the third dimension. This personal development—or evolution—is in our consciousness. However, I also believe that as an individual evolves to higher levels of consciousness, such levels bring awareness of the interconnectedness of all life, and with it, an expanded circle of care and concern for others. This awareness brings a desire to serve others, a desire that seems natural from the viewpoint that we are all one. This intent to serve others frequently includes a desire to assist others in the expansion of their consciousness. Therefore, in this light, one person's evolution assists the group' s consciousness. Also, we might consider that an individual's consciousness is part of the collective consciousness of all humanity, so that one's growth contributes to everyone's growth in that regard.

Must we really take an active role in our personal evolution? Won't we just naturally "transcend the third dimension" when our bodies experience the process of death?

According to some spiritual teachers, the transition from this life to our next experience allows us to automatically release the limitations imposed upon us by our identification with our bodies and our sense of separation from one another. Yet, these same teachers typically maintain that some sense of personal identity is carried with us into our next level of expression. Although the release of the body may bring an expansion of our awareness, such expansion doesn't eliminate the necessity for growth during our time in the third dimension. As I see it, the greater our growth in the third dimension, the more benefit we experience overall. The greater our wisdom at the point of transition (commonly called "death"), the greater the potential opportunity for enhanced assimilation of our new expanded awareness. In addition, if (as some spiritual teachers and traditions suggest) reincarnation back into the third dimension reoccurs until we learn our lessons here, then having greater wisdom at the point of transition brings with it an increased likelihood that we have "completed" our experience here.

Then what must each of us do to transcend the third dimension and evolve personally?

The simple answer is be aware of this process, set an intention to further your evolution, create a vision of your personal evolution, and act in a manner that is in alignment with that vision. Your vision and related actions must incorporate all aspects of your life: your inner work and outer work (that is, your work on yourself and your work in relation to others). I find philosopher Ken Wilber's integral practice helpful for understanding the various parts of one's life in which you need to consider your plan for growth. Working on your shadow-self is essential. Some type of spiritual practice that builds within you an awareness of the oneness of life is key. Other spiritual teachers frequently offer other specific guidance. My suggestion is that we use logic to build our plan, but that we also use the vast power of our intuition to choose the path that is best for us individually. Later chapters of the book will provide specific guidance on personal evolution, which may be helpful in creating your personal plan.

That's the simple answer?

Yes. It sounds simple, but that doesn't make it easy. And there is a more complex piece to our evolution that we need to consider: Our physical nature has evolved through the third dimension for thousands of years. That process has hardwired within us certain factors that have served us along our evolutionary path but now create barriers as we seek to evolve further. Some consider these factors to be coded into our DNA; others say they are part of our

11

collective consciousness. Either way, these structures keep us with one foot firmly planted in the third dimension, even as we feel called to higher levels of awareness.

What are some of these structures that have served us but now limit us?

There are parts of humanity's choices and behavior that obviously can be considered animalistic in nature. Let's consider Abraham Maslow's Hierarchy of Needs. At the lowest level we seek to meet basic physiological needs such as obtaining air, water, and food. As we meet those needs, we are able to focus upon our desire for basic safety and security: shelter, procreation to continue the species, and so forth. Maslow points out that next we will seek to create a sense of belonging with others and a desire to experience love. We must consider that for thousands of years, meeting each of these needs served an evolutionary purpose: Humanity continued to live, thrive, and reproduce. Yet our hardwiring to meet these needs keeps us stuck in sensing the need to compete against others for what appear to be limited resources (food, water, land, money, sexual partners, power, possessions that make life easier, etcetera). Although at some level we may be called to transcend these desires, our third-dimensional hardwiring keeps bringing us back to them.

How do we overcome this hardwiring?

It comes back to this simple answer: through awareness, intention, vision, and action. If we are not aware of how our third-dimensional evolutionary process has created these gifts and challenges, we will continue to ignore the challenges rather than address them. We will continue to live our lives in competition and struggle, seeking to fill the bottomless pit of needs that can never be satisfied, keeping our attention and focus on lack and limitation and creating more of the same.

Is there anything else we need to understand in moving beyond the third dimension?

Yes, there are several things. First, we need to understand what many mystics and philosophers have pointed out: the creative power of our thoughts—that thoughts are things. Evolution has allowed consciousness to make a critical leap within humanity: We have become aware of the fact that we are aware. With that, these mystics and philosophers have described how we are beginning to move into an awareness that the consciousness embedded within us is actually the creative power of the Divine, and that through our free will-choice we can use that power for destructive purposes or creative purposes. We need to learn to harness the vast power within us for good, for ourselves and for others.

It's hard for me to believe that my thoughts have creative power. I have so many personal experiences of thinking about something that I didn't manifest.

Yes, I understand. We will further examine this topic later in this book. But for now, I would simply ask you to consider how most of the things that you have consciously created in your life began first as a thought. Somewhere within your personal beliefs, you at least accept that there is some creative power within thinking.

13

What else would be useful for us to understand in moving beyond the third dimension?

Next, we need to remember the truth that we are interrelated to everyone else. We need to grasp that on an intellectual level, and then embody it into our emotions and choices. We need to release our attachment to all the trappings of the third dimension. To be clear, yes, let's enjoy the vast array of beauty and bounty of life here on planet Earth. It truly is a gift. But attachments to all that is here will keep us stuck here. Finally, we need to be aware of the evolutionary process and our role in it. We need to recognize that we are conscious co-creators in the process. As we grow and evolve personally, we need to consider how we might use the power of our thoughts and intentions for the greater good of all so that we not only complete our individual third-dimensional experience but assist others on their path as well.

So are we really continuing to evolve?

Yes, I believe so. The process of physical evolution obviously is still occurring on Earth. But as I mentioned previously, this evolution as it relates to humanity is occurring more in our consciousness than on the physical level. In our evolution, we become more aware—more *enlightened*. Hence, evolution's next step for us is in consciousness, awareness, and enlightenment.

Where does religion or spirituality fit into this?

In my opinion, religion represents the formalized rules, dogma, and organizations that evolved to point humanity back towards this divine unity. In that regard, religions have served a useful purpose. Yet they are tainted by humanity's animalistic base needs and thus have limited us by simultaneously dividing us and keeping us separate from one another. One must consider this: Does a religion's emphasis of its rules, its sacred texts, the specialness of its group, its discouragement of marriage outside the group, and its claim of being the path that is "the only way to God" serve to unite us as a people or divide us? More often than not, such thinking engenders more divisiveness and less love. Such characteristics of religion have even encouraged violence and war. Is this the next logical step for humanity? Is this our highest possibility as a people?

Spirituality, on the other hand, implies a direct experience of unity. Spirituality seeks for us to have a direct link to the Divine without any intermediary. Religion may have served our evolutionary past, but it is spirituality that will take us to the next level in the future. Spiritual practices such as prayer and meditation seek to create within us our own personal experience of God. Such experience moves us into higher levels of care and concern for our fellow humans, as well as assisting us in releasing attachments to third-dimensional desires. Hence, a routine spiritual practice of communing with a sense greater than our smallness is essential to transcending the third dimension.

As our personal evolution unfolds and we become more aware of our interrelationship to everyone, how does that relate to the collective evolution of humanity?

As we as individuals evolve or grow in consciousness or become enlightened (however you prefer to describe the process), we become more aware and truly embody the reality that we are all interconnected—that we are all part of some grand "oneness." As that occurs, it is inevitable that we will grow in our sense of love and concern for all our fellow beings. This is one area where religions have served us. There is a common thread in all faiths that teaches the Golden Rule: Do unto others as you would have them do onto you. This call to ethical behavior served us early in our evolutionary process, as we banded together in tribes and cities and countries. The more we all cooperated within "our group," the more the group flourished. Yet, the Golden Rule's guidance was never limited to any one group. As we expand our sense of "the other" to greater and greater degrees, soon it envelops all humanity, all life, the planet, and ultimately the universe in total. What would it mean to treat every person on the planet as we would wish to be treated? What would it mean if we treated the planet and the universe as we would wish to be treated?

There certainly is plenty of evidence that we do not treat one another or the planet as we would like to be treated. What do you think it would be like if we did?

I suspect most of us could agree on many of the characteristics of such a world, but obviously there is no consensus. I have my vision of what such a world might look like. First, each person would have access to the basic rights as outlined by the goals of the United Nations (access to adequate water, food, education, to be treated with dignity and respect, and to be able to live with certain freedoms). Yet beyond that, each person would have a reverence for all life—as we look outward, we would see ourselves in other people, in animals, in plants—we would sense our connectedness. Yes, we would continue to seek to meet our basic needs for our own lives. But there would be greater awareness where our continued efforts to meet our needs crossed over into the territory of meeting "wants and desires" (the things we endeavor to attain that in the big picture we don't really "need"). There is nothing wrong with meeting wants and desires. Experiencing the fullness of life in the third dimension is one of the gifts of being here. Our full experience of the infinite variety of life here is one of the main reasons we were placed here. Through us, Spirit or Infinite Consciousness experiences the richness of this physical domain. However, our expanded awareness of meeting wants and desires would bring knowledge of when our efforts crossed into harming others. There is goodness in meeting our needs, wants, and desires as long as they express life. When our efforts cause harm, they no longer express life.

Could you give some specific examples of when meeting our wants and desires can cause harm and no longer express life?

First I'll present some larger, global examples. Consider the actions of Wall Street financiers, whose desire for greater profits for their company caused harm to individual homeowners as well as to our collective economy. Consider the Gulf of Mexico oil spill, where the combination of our government's desire to increase domestic oil production as well as the oil company's desire to maximize profits led to cutting corners and an ultimate ecological disaster. Consider the ongoing violence in the Middle East, which is tied to the self-interest of particular countries and religions.

17

In each of these cases, some group is attempting to meet its wants and desires that are beyond the level of basic needs. And in each case, such efforts crossed over into harming other people or the environment.

At this point, these groups and individuals no longer were "expressing life" in its greatest expression. If the decision-makers in each of these cases had stopped to ask themselves, "What action can we take that will serve the greatest number?" or "What can we do to meet our needs that will cause no harm?", would they have made the choices they did? If they were truly treating others as they wished to be treated, different choices would have been made. To be clear, my point here with these examples is not to debate any specific governmental or corporate political decision. Rather, I am simply suggesting that in a possible world where all humanity lives by the Golden Rule, where the "other" they are "doing onto" is everyone and everything, there would have been other decisions, actions, and outcomes.

To create that world, doesn't it start with each one of us?

Absolutely! Each of us should examine our own lives to find examples where we might not be living by the Golden Rule. Do you ever cut someone off on the highway because you're in a hurry to get where you want to go? Do you ever gossip or bad-mouth someone because they don't think or act like you want them to? Do you ever ignore someone's request for help because for some reason you're mad at them? Do you ever forward some viral but untruthful e-mail because it makes a political statement you happen to favor? Do you ever judge others negatively because they are different from you: a different race, religion, sexual orientation, etcetera? The point is, every day we make choices. Are our choices in alignment with doing onto others as we would wish to be treated? As each of us grows in our personal awareness, we will sense and know how we are each stewards of this planet in the third dimension, as well as caretakers and teachers for those continuing to struggle. It does not serve the collective good for us to stay mired in the third dimension, but rather it serves the greater good for us to grow and become enlightened. The more of us that move into that place in our consciousness, the greater the collective evolution of humanity.

In what ways are we "collectively evolving"?

We are growing collectively inwardly and outwardly. Inwardly, we are evolving at a cultural level, as well as in our collective consciousness. Outwardly, we might consider that our global systems—the outward expression of society, such as our technology and ability to tap the collective "global brain"—are also evolving.

How are we evolving culturally?

This is where I find the model of Spiral Dynamics so helpful. The data that supports this theory shows that humanity is evolving through a series of worldviews. As we meet our individual needs in our current world conditions, using a particular outlook on life (that is, a *worldview*), we evolve into new world conditions with new needs, which require a new worldview. We develop through the same sequence of worldviews in our individual lives (from birth up to our current status). At a collective level, humanity has evolved through the same sequence (from our caveman days through the present). Humanity's earliest worldviews were centered on meeting base needs similar to Maslow's theory: safety and survival, banding together in tribes, and so forth.

Although these early worldviews still exist in some areas of the planet, currently there are three predominant worldviews that came more recently out of humanity's history. These are, in evolutionary order: (1) a traditional view from which our major religions and legal systems arose; (2) a modern view from which science, capitalism and democracy arose; and, (3) a more recent, postmodern viewpoint characterized by a belief in equal rights and environmental movements. We will further examine this theory later in the book.

Ultimately, Spiral Dynamics as well as similar models such as Integral Theory, point to our evolving to even higher levels of individual and group awareness, where we are able to recognize and value the interplay of all the other levels. Interestingly, some of the characteristics at these higher levels of awareness include such factors as the melding of science and spirituality, recognizing the interconnectedness and systems interplay of everything on the planet, and an awareness of a greater unity of all. These are characteristics that mystics often describe as coming at higher levels of awareness. Although Spiral Dynamics data shows that much of humanity still has one of the earlier worldviews, the theory points the way to our evolutionary future and shows that growing numbers of people are headed toward these higher worldviews.

What do you mean by "collective consciousness" and how is it evolving?

Just as we have an individual consciousness, all of our individual consciousnesses feed one group consciousness for all of humanity. Swiss psychotherapist Carl Jung wrote extensively about the collective consciousness. What many have realized is that not only does our individual consciousness provide input into humanity's collective consciousness, but that this greater consciousness is tapped into by each of our subconscious minds, providing silent input into our thoughts and choices. The group mind, in a sense, serves to limit us and what we see as possible. As each of us grow individually, we feed a greater level of potential for all humanity into this group consciousness, raising the bar on what is considered possible for all of us.

And what about outward evidence of our evolution?

In spite of all the challenges our planet currently faces, there is plenty of evidence that we are moving into a world where humanity senses at a greater level our interconnectedness and our related expanded sense of care and concern for each other. The Internet and related phenomena, such as the rise of social media websites, connects us with each other globally and immediately. There is a rising trend in corporations to be considered successful by the combination of profits and social responsibility. There is an increased tendency by individuals later in life to release careers that brought material success and move into "work" that feeds their soul. There is a rise in the number of nonprofit groups whose mission is to enhance life conditions for everyone around the planet. The United Nations continues

21

to promote the meeting of certain basic human needs as a "right" through such efforts as their Millennium Development Goals, which are designed to end poverty and hunger around the planet. These and similar examples indicate that we are moving forward in our evolution.

What is our role in contributing to such evolution?

Hopefully by now it's clear: The collective consciousness of humanity evolves by our personal evolution. Humanity's cultural and societal evolution moves forward by our personal growth. Each of us has a responsibility to answer that inner call that asks us to transcend our limits and grow to the greatest levels of possibility for our lives. Our growth occurs in our consciousness inwardly and in our actions outwardly. We previously mentioned that each of us should set our intention toward our highest possibility for our lives, to create a vision of what that looks like and then to act in alignment with that vision. We also mentioned using logic and intuition to create our individual plan, as well as some components the plan should contain.

Considering our collective evolution, we must add one additional aspect to our plan: service to others. There are so many issues facing our planet at this time that it's easy to get overwhelmed and do nothing. Let go of that feeling. Pick one issue that you are passionate about, and then act to do something to address it, no matter how small the action. Add this service action to all your other personal aspects of your plan for growth. The combination of our individual actions, coupled with their igniting cascading change through the "butterfly effect," will truly make a difference. Hold firm in the knowledge that to the degree that we all grow individually to transcend the third dimension, that growth supports the collective growth of all.

We sort of assume here that we wish to transcend the third dimension. Is this true?

That's an individual decision for each of us to make, based on experience and our own free will-choice. I believe that ultimately more and more of us will become enlightened and realize the importance of transcending this school and playground of space and time. There may always be some who will choose to move through the third dimension, but in the vast expanse of time as experienced in the third dimension, I believe those numbers will diminish.

Any final thoughts?

Yes. One aspect of our being human is that we learn and grow by the dual gifts of our intellect and intuition. We listen to our heads and to our hearts. The thoughts expressed in this chapter were intended to be presented in a logical, easy-to-understand manner that would feed your intellect. But beyond that, I hope that as your intellect resonated with these ideas, it also opened your heart.

French philosopher, paleontologist, and Jesuit priest Pierre Teilhard de Chardin wrote about the evolution of humanity and our path as we move upward in consciousness. He described the melding of individual human minds into one global mind called the *noosphere*. As our consciousness grew beyond that, he pointed to what he called the "Omega point"—some point in the future that is pulling all creation toward it. So let us consider this: Spirit or Ultimate Consciousness divided itself up in awareness and embedded itself in all of life so that we could experience individuality and free will-choice as we simultaneously moved upward, following the laws of evolution. This evolutionary track involved smaller pockets of consciousness coming together in greater pockets of consciousness, until in humanity here on Earth (and perhaps elsewhere) such consciousness crossed a threshold into self-awareness. Our personal, individual pocket of consciousness is now being pulled by the process of evolution to combine with others at an even higher level of awareness that we can only imagine.

What is this Omega point that is pulling us upward and onward so that we might ultimately transcend the third dimension? What force can we imagine that seeks to pull us out from our sense of separation from one another and desires to connect us in our awareness with others? What force could that be? Teilhard de Chardin wrote, "Someday, after mastering the winds, the waves, the tides and gravity, we shall harness for God the energies of love, and then, for a second time in the history of the world, man will have discovered fire." That force is *love*. Spirit embedded in us consciousness and love. It was love that placed us here in the third dimension. It is love that is calling us home.

Chapter Two

Science's Story: Big History

Now, we leave the self-dialogue approach for a more straightforward style. In this chapter, we continue our evolutionary theme as we look at the growing concept within academia of something called "Big History." It's my belief that the development of this multidisciplinary approach to our past, present, and future is the academic world's way of attempting to place some meaning and greater understanding to our overall human story.

Humanity has long sought to understand its place in history and creation by telling itself a story as to how everything began and how we got here. Generally, every group of humans since the beginning of recorded history has had some type of creation story. For eons our creation stories essentially came from religious myths. Over time, such mythical stories and their deeper meanings were collapsed in our tellings down to literal truths. For a long time, the most well-known Western creation story was the biblical tale of Adam and Eve.

Then science came along and showed that these stories could not be literally true. In this transition, our understanding of the word *myth* also changed—the term losing its original connotation where mythical stories contained truth that could not always be expressed in words and logic, and instead becoming a term that essentially meant *fairytale*. Some individuals (such as writers Thomas Berry and Brian Swimme) have suggested that humanity has suffered by not having an adequate replacement creation story. Big History stepped in to fill that void.

Now, I recognize that many of you who read through the dialogue in the first chapter might have a hard time accepting some of the ideas presented. Concepts such as our being an expression of multiplicity within the unity of spirit, and consciousness being the ground of all being, may be hard to intellectually accept as true—especially if this is the first time you've considered them. That's why I find Big History useful. It's a scientific and academic way of reorienting our thinking along the massive timeline of humanity. And, it's a great springboard for moving into considering more metaphysical possibilities regarding our evolution. If this brief introduction resonates with you, I encourage you to seek out the more detailed material.

Science replaced the fairytales with a new story of the Big Bang and physical evolution. There's a lot of scientific evidence to support the new story. The problem is that the new story is void of meaning. It may explain the *how* but it is silent on the *why*. Why did the Big Bang occur? Why is there an evolutionary process? Why is there life? Why is there consciousness? Science may have given humanity a more accurate story based on the facts, but the scientific story has not filled humanity's eternal need for meaning. Big History is the closest approach to filling this need that has come out of the scientific academic world.

I was first introduced to the concept of Big History through a company called "The Great Courses," which offered a college class titled "Big History: the Big Bang, Life on Earth, and the Rise of Humanity." The course was taught by Professor David Christian of San Diego State University. Christian is also the author of the book called *Maps of Time*, which introduces the same concepts. I highly recommend the course. Apparently, Bill Gates does too. He is funding an initiative to make the course available to high school students and others for free. (Check it out at https://course.bighistoryproject.com/)

What is Big History? Basically it's a story of the history of Earth, going back to the Big Bang and bringing the story forward to the present and into the near future. Most history courses that we took in school focused on human history, primarily those major events for which we have written records. Big History, on the other hand, draws from many sources of study. These include cosmology, biology, geology, human history, and more. Hence Big History takes a very high-level approach, from which we can draw very big trends on the direction of Earth's evolution.

Christian not only tells the "story" of Big History, but also explains how we *know* the story. He gives concise descriptions of how science has determined this to be our best picture of how we got to where we are. If you're interested in how science knows this story, you may want to listen to Christian's course. Here, I will briefly run through the general story at a very, very high-level, to give you a sense of it.

Big History begins a millisecond after the Big Bang. That's interesting, because science offers no answers for what might have been in existence before the Big Bang, or why the Big Bang occurred. Science simply says that the best evidence shows that there was a Big Bang, and when it happened (approximately 1400 million years ago).

Science says that all matter was compressed into a very small area and that some event caused it to explode out in all directions very quickly. One of the interesting things about this broader view of the past is that it paints a picture of things "emerging" at just the right time and in just the right way for the Big History story to unfold. Although the story shows a picture of many, many emergent properties, there are major ones that Christian labels *thresholds*. These thresholds were changes of such monumental proportion that we could look back and see how the universe was critically changed from what existed before to what existed afterward. The Big Bang was obviously the first such threshold.

Science says that all the forces that we now understand to control matter within the universe (gravity, electromagnetic forces, etcetera) existed right after the Big Bang. Again, they could have existed before the Big Bang, but science does not go back that far. The Big Bang created a kind of primordial soup of matter that was lumpy. If the distribution of matter had been totally even in its distribution, there might not have been any further evolution. However, the lumpiness, combined with gravity, began to grow the smaller "lumps" into larger and larger forms. The first forms were the elements of hydrogen and helium. Eventually, as these lumps of hydrogen and helium grew larger, this process ultimately created the first stars. The emergence of stars is Christian's second major threshold.

Over time, gravity brought the elements into increasingly larger and increasingly hotter masses. Gravity brought stars together into galaxies. Within the process of stars heating up, the first basic elements beyond hydrogen and helium eventually were created. The best evidence we have says that the process of stars expanding and contracting through their life cycle created all the elements that we recognize. It is science's understanding that the heavier elements were made in the death throes of large stars collapsing into themselves under great pressure and then breaking up and dispersing themselves throughout the universe. The creation of chemical elements is Christian's third emergent threshold.

As these elements floated around in space, gravity brought them together in the form of planets, asteroids, and other space bodies. Over time, the gravitational field of stars, combined with the gravity contained within the larger lumps of elements themselves, created (over a very long time) the planets and their orbits. The creation of the Earth and the solar system was Christian's fourth emergent threshold.

Again, through millions of years and various processes, there were changes upon the Earth. The oceans were formed, land was created, and our atmosphere developed. Somewhere along the way, life emerged. This was Christian's fifth major threshold.

Although not considered separate key "thresholds" by Christian, there are three other distinctive "emergent" properties that came about with the emergence of life. They are metabolism, reproduction, and adaptation. Metabolism is an entity's ability to use and process energy from the environment. Consider how most plants absorb sunlight and transform it for their own growth. Or, consider how animals digest plants or other animals in order to process the energy contained in them. Reproduction is an entity's ability to re-create itself—splitting itself in two, or the process of sexual reproduction. Adaptation is an entity's ability to change over time in response to changes in the environment.

Obviously, evolution is an integral part of Big History. Christian goes into great detail over the story of Darwin and how he created the theory of natural selection. You probably remember the basics from your biology class: inheritability, mutation and gene variation, adaptation and natural selection, and finally, "survival of the fittest."

Plants and animals reproduce themselves, passing to their offspring the basic characteristics of the parents. There are two factors that can lead to their young not being identical. One factor is that in sexual reproduction, the offspring inherits half its genes from one parent and the other half from the other parent. The other factor is that genes sometimes *mutate*, introducing random changes. Hence, there continually is the emergence of newness within species.

Life always reproduces more offspring than can survive, based on limited resources. Those aspects of life best suited to the environment live longer and reproduce more, passing on to their offspring their characteristics. Over time, this process favors examples of life that best fit the current environment. There is a continuous interplay between life and the environment, as each changes the other.

Although Big History goes into some detail regarding the evolution of species, for our purposes here, we will simply note that over millions of years, life continued to evolve on Earth until early humanoids were created. Eventually, the sixth threshold was crossed when humanity emerged.

Since the emergence of humans was seen as a major change, Christian considers the question *what makes humans different?* That's an interesting question, and he answers it differently from what I have heard previously.

When I was growing up, the story I was told was about what set people apart from lower species was that people were the first and only animals to use tools. The human development of language and communication also was seen as an essential difference. Science has gone on to disprove that humanity is the sole user of tools; therefore, that doesn't seem to be frequently used anymore as the line of demarcation. And, it appears that other species can communicate, and in some cases exhibit rudimentary language abilities.

Another way I had heard of answering the question relates to our level of consciousness. Ernest Holmes, the 13th-century Persian poet Rumi, and other mystics often point to the fact that it is because humans "know that they know" that they are different from other forms of life. In other words, the fact that we became self-aware, a characteristic not previously in existence, is seen as an important threshold crossed by humanity.

For Christian, what makes humans different is their ability to transfer learning from one person to another and across generations. This ability to benefit from the knowledge of our ancestors and to know all that they learned is what he says makes us unique. Yes, this relates to our use of language and our state of internal awareness. But from a Big History perspective, it is the use of that language and the awareness through conveying our wisdom that has set us apart and fostered the tremendous success of human achievements.

After the rise of humanity, the Big History course does a very quick run-through of human history, showing how we build greater and greater degrees of complexity in our organizational structures and our technology. Along the way, we cross more major thresholds in the story. The seventh threshold was when humans began to leave their early nomadic lifestyle and settle down at one location through the development of agricultural methods. The eighth threshold occurred with the "modern revolution" that included four key changes: accelerating innovation, the formation of larger and more complex societies, the movement into a global society, and the growing human impact on the biosphere.

One interesting side note from the course that I found fascinating is this: Humanity is the first species that uses more energy than it needs for basic life and survival. Other species, as well as early man, used only as much energy as they needed to survive and reproduce. The history of humanity shows that we used more and more energy per person as life became more complex. It's interesting to contemplate how much energy it really takes for us to navigate through modern life.

Ultimately, Big History courses still steer away from topics such as where we came from, why everything exists, and where we are going in the future. However, its high-level view of universal history does assist those who are steeped in a scientific worldview to expand their vision and see humanity's history through a larger and more inclusive lens. It's a great introductory way of shifting towards those questions of meaning.

Chapter Three

The Emergence of Consciousness

In Chapter One, I noted that our future evolution would be primarily within consciousness. In Chapter Two, one of the major thresholds mentioned in Big History was when humanity developed such a degree of consciousness we were able to learn about life and pass that learning on to others. But that raises the question, what exactly is consciousness?

That question has been considered by philosophers and others since the beginning of recorded history. Wikipedia online encyclopedia defines consciousness as "the quality or state of being aware of an external object or something within oneself. It has been defined as: sentience, awareness, subjectivity, the ability to experience or to feel, wakefulness, having a sense of selfhood, and the executive control system of the mind." There are many theories as to where consciousness comes from and what it is, but ultimately it is one of the greatest mysteries of human understanding.

There are various theories concerning the development of consciousness and mind, all leading to questions such as how our consciousness interacts with our brain. This also has been called "the mind-body problem" or "the hard problem of consciousness": How can outer experiences, which enter our bodies through our senses, give rise to phenomenal experiences? We can explain how light hits a flower, and how some wavelengths are absorbed by the flower and some bounce on to our retina, where the light triggers reactions that send nerve signals to certain areas of our brain. We cannot explain how we sense in our consciousness "red flowers."

Some philosophers and scientists offered dualistic explanations—that consciousness is one thing and matter is another, with the rules of science not necessarily applying to consciousness. Others have offered monistic explanations —that is there is only "one stuff," which serves to bypass the hard problem that comes with dualistic reasoning. Some monists (including Buddhists) say there is only consciousness and that all matter is ultimately an illusion. Other monists (including many current-day materialistic scientists) say there is only matter, and that consciousness somehow comes from it. Still others (such as William James, Bertrand Russell, and David Chalmers) offer a viewpoint called *neutral monism*, which considers matter and consciousness to simply be two different ways of expressing the same underlying element. Neutral monism is related to the philosophical concept of *panpsychism*, which espouses that "mind" is "everywhere."

Traditional evolutionary science offers good explanations as to how animals developed complex nervous systems with coordinating brains. Adaptation gives a good description for the evolution of the human brain. But then we have to stop and consider the question, "Is the brain the same thing as the mind?" Your answer will relate to which of the theories of consciousness you believe. As most materialistic scientists believe there is only matter, most believe that the brain and the mind are the same.

Hence, the evolutionary explanations for the development of our brains offer clues as to the development of the mind and consciousness. Some believe that consciousness is simply an irrelevant byproduct of the evolution of our brain. Others believe that conscious awareness had some evolutionary advantage offering us greater "fitness" for our environment.

However, such explanations don't adequately tell us how consciousness arose, if our belief revolves around dualism, idealism (that only consciousness is real) or neutral monism. Traditional evolutionary theory can explain the "matter" side of the brain's development in dualism, but you're still stuck with the hard problem! In idealism, consciousness was always there—we just are experiencing an illusion of evolution! In neutral monism (and panpsychism), mind has always existed and consciousness was always present, and the process of evolution has allowed our awareness of it to come into play. Obviously, this theory is the one that most closely relates to the evolutionary story offered in this book.

For those who find these theories interesting, the Resources section of this book provides recommended books and articles. You can make up your own mind as to which theory makes the most sense. For now, I simply want you to consider your own personal experience of consciousness and offer you a way of looking at that experience through that "evolutionary lens" I mentioned in the Introduction.

Imagine this: You and I are little "pockets of consciousness," and we are walking around with our stories of who and what we are. We recall a past with our parents, our friends, our schooling, our culture, and the sum total is our life story that we cling to. I have my story; you have your story. We bump into each other and interact, adjusting our story with the new experience. And so it goes....

Our moment-to-moment experience of our consciousness can vary in its qualities. We can be alert and focused. We can be tired and sleepy. We can be feeling the effects of drugs. We can be unconscious or asleep. We can be experiencing the dream state.

We can use the pattern of our experiences to form an underlying belief about how the world works and what is ultimately true. We sense within us the unique and individual totality of our personal story that is different but somehow similar to the stories of others. I have my experience of my consciousness and hold a belief that you have generally a very comparable experience, even though I know that your unique experiences have led you to having your own unique stories and beliefs.

What's your story?

But are you truly this individual and separate consciousness that you tell yourself you are, while believing that I am this other individual and separate consciousness? Or could it be that you, I, and everyone else are part of some *collective consciousness*?

Here's the real truth in my belief system: Consciousness is more than all the people walking around telling themselves their story! Consciousness is not simply a byproduct of the firing of neurons in the brain. Consciousness is not simply that inner world of your thoughts and emotions that you sense.

I want you to consider consciousness differently. I want

you to see it as an *intelligent energy* that is embedded in and flows through everything, everywhere. This energy is in every atom, every molecule, everything…. Then I invite you to consider that consciousness (or *mind* or *energy*) builds up in complexity as it is grows from being embedded in the smallest things, to those smaller things joining together to form the largest things—with humans somewhere in the middle of this chain!

So think on this: As stuff grows in complexity (from atoms and molecules to plants and animals to planets and stars), it contains more and more (and deeper) consciousness. This process of growing in complexity, we know by the name *evolution*. Rocks have consciousness, but as they are not very complex, neither is the level of their "mind." Hence, their intelligence is very limited as compared with higher forms. Plants have higher degrees of complexity and higher levels of consciousness. The levels of animals are even higher, and humanity is higher still.

At some point, as the entity's complexity becomes great enough, the depth of the consciousness crosses the threshold into a state of self-awareness—and then "it knows that it knows," as does humanity. Maybe other species, such as dolphins, have crossed this threshold as well. Perhaps the buildup of complexity on other planets has allowed other species in the universe to do the same. That idea seems very reasonable to me.

But even though all the stuff of the universe is embedded with consciousness, we must not lose sight of the fact that all of this intelligence is linked in one unity. At some level above us—and growing in awareness within humanity—there is an awareness of the interconnectedness of everything. This awareness springs from the interconnectedness of consciousness and is fueled by the evolutionary force of love.

Think about the level of awareness of the cells in our bodies. They have consciousness, but not to the degree that the whole consciousness that your "collective you" has. Your individual cells cannot comprehend the unity of your body as you do. Imagine that you are those cells, and that above you is a greater awareness and interconnectedness that you are not privy to. If you had the higher awareness, you would be aware of the greater unity.

For now, simply remember that as you walk around thinking you are just this individual little pocket of consciousness with a story it tells itself about who it is, its true identity is a sum of the consciousness embedded in it. Our "individual collective consciousness" is part of some greater whole that we glimpse only occasionally.

That's a much bigger story and a much bigger pocket of consciousness than we generally think we are! In fact, you are part of something so big that most of us have a hard time wrapping our mind or imagination around the idea.

Previously, we considered that the cells in our body have an intelligence or mind that directs their activities, but at their level of awareness they cannot sense the level of mind/consciousness/awareness that we carry around in our human existence each day. A drop of blood has no concept of our collective awareness of our entirety as a human.

Similarly, we have a hard time limiting our perception to what it might be like to be a drop of blood. It has been said that our brain works like a screening tool, filtering out of our awareness all of the sensory input that is available. Most of the business of our bodies is carried out automatically, without our conscious awareness. Yet it has been shown that, with training, we can exert conscious control over those functions. Our human consciousness is tied to the consciousness of lower bodily functioning. Similarly, our brains also limit the flow of external sensory data into our awareness. We hear and see only a small sliver of the spectrums of sound and light. Can you imagine what your consciousness would be like if you had in your awareness all the awareness of all of your internal cells as well as all the flow of external sensory input around us? Neither can I.

But just as you are made up of smaller aspects of consciousness, your consciousness and your experiences feed the knowledge and intelligence of a still higher awareness. Many suggest that this higher awareness might exist in intermediate levels such as "the collective consciousness of all humans" or Gaia (the consciousness of the planet Earth). But most mystics tell us that ultimately our awareness feeds and is connected to the collective experiences of Spirit at the highest level: the totality of all that is.

This experience of our lives at the collective level (by Spirit or God) is what we have referenced as "multiplicity in the unity." There is unity at the highest level, but it is experienced as multiplicity as we humans" knock around in life," telling ourselves that we are separate and apart from everything.

Consider this: If you were God or Spirit and could experience everything completely, to have the greatest experience possible, you might have to take your awareness and "divide it up" into parts that were not aware that they were part of the whole. And, you might have to take these individual aspects of yourself that had forgotten and "stretch them out" so that they would experience time and space. And, you might have to give them the ability to make "free-will choices" so that you wouldn't already have predetermined the experience as they play around in time and space. By doing this, you wouldn't know exactly what was going to happen, and you would have an infinitely more varied experience than if you had not created this scenario.

Of course, even though Spirit allowed the flow of consciousness to "forget" that it is a part of Spirit, Spirit did keep itself as the ultimate "sensor" of all experiences. Spirit receives the collective experiences of everything, everywhere, while we are in a state of forgetfulness. But all is not lost! We are also in a state of "re-minding"—of coming back, of returning. As we evolve in complexity and deepen in consciousness, we begin awakening to the truth of our connectedness. We remember where we came from—and through the force of love, drawing us out and sensing our connectedness to things and people and events outside us, we deepen in our sense of Oneness with everything. We go back to Spirit.

As we walk around each day, we may tell ourselves stories about who and what we are. When we come from our lower levels of awareness, our stories are mired in the world of effects and separation. When we come from our higher levels, our stories shift toward unity. Let us lift our heads upwards towards "heaven" (a sense of Oneness) and live our lives seeing our Truth, our Beauty, our Perfection, our Oneness. That is our charge each day, to move our attention to the higher levels of our consciousness. It is our goal. It is our calling.

But now, let's look at this consciousness from a different perspective. If the Power and Presence that created the universe—that ultimate "Source" that is Mind and Consciousness—that created this field of Mind and Consciousness in which we move and of which we became aware as we crossed a mental threshold—if this Power is in everything, then it is in us. Through our use of consciousness or mind, we have access to a great creative power.

In Chapter One, I offered the idea that our thoughts have creative power. I recognize that many of us have difficulty accepting that fact because we have so much personal experience that argues against it's being true. We have all pictured some desired experience in our mind and it didn't occur; therefore we have empirical evidence that our thoughts are not creative. But on the other hand, I suspect that all of us also have had the opposite experience: where we thought of something and it manifested. So which is it? Do our thoughts have power, and if so, why does it appear that that power is so inconsistent?

By now most people know about the "Law of Attraction", based upon the popularity of the movie and book, *The Secret*, which discuss it in detail. Many long-time students of metaphysics were pleased to see how the movie and book generated interest in a concept they have long studied. Yet many of us felt that the movie had two basic limitations. First, it focused too much on creating material wealth over the true spiritual purpose of the law. Secondly, it glossed over certain aspects of the law that, when not understood, can lead to failure and disillusionment with its truth. My goal in the next few paragraphs is to simplify the Law of Attraction, as well as to correct some of its misunderstandings.

Let's begin by considering again that the universe is made up of energy and matter, which are interchangeable with one another, and that both respond to certain laws. Science purports that as far back as a few milliseconds after the Big Bang energy, matter, and these laws were in existence. Science and its materialistic approach tends to limit its study to laws involving matter (laws with effects that can easily be seen and measured). Other laws (such as the Law of Attraction) that involve nonmaterial things are either dismissed as impossible or are considered disproven because experiments involving them cannot consistently be replicated.

Simply stated, the Law of Attraction says that what we tend to think about manifests in the material world. We often hear the phrase "thoughts are things." Hence, a beginning student of the Law of Attraction would be led to believe that so long as they "think" something enough they will see it manifest in their lives. Sometimes that happens, and validates the law. Other times, they don't get what they think about and end up believing that the law is a bunch of bunk.

Generally speaking, there are three reasons why people don't get what they consciously think about. The first reason is that we must not only think something consistently, but we must act and speak in a manner that is in alignment with what we think. We can affirm and affirm and affirm until we're blue in the face, but if we are acting in a manner inconsistent with our affirmations, then we will not see the desired manifestation. If you are thinking and affirming that a new and wonderful relationship is flowing into your life, yet you stay home and never put yourself out where you can be open to being a friend to other people, than you will never see the manifestation of relationships that may be waiting for you. There's an old joke that you can affirm to win the lottery all you want, but for that desire to manifest, you first have to buy a ticket.

The second reason we may not see a manifestation of our thoughts is because we forget that our thoughts have two parts to them. The first part is that of which we are consciously aware. This is the part of consciousness we use when we are *trying* to employ the Law of Attraction through our affirmations. This is the part that people know about, and when they don't manifest what they are consciously thinking, they then assume that the Law of Attraction doesn't work. The second aspect of our thinking (and the one we tend to forget is at play) is the part that is below the level of our awareness. We have developed patterns of thinking throughout our lives that have become so ingrained that we often don't realize they exist. These "thoughts" are below the level of awareness—they are the source of our beliefs, generate our habits, and lead to our emotions. Simply stated, if we consciously think one thing, but subconsciously believe another, then we will not see the desires of our conscious thoughts manifest.

Let's take an advanced metaphysics aside for a moment. Author and philosopher Christian de Quincy, in his recent book, *Consciousness From Zombies to Angels*, challenges the notion that thoughts create our reality. However, he goes on to add that may be a matter of semantics. He asserts that when people use the word *thought* in this context, they really mean *consciousness*. He points out that "a great deal of consciousness goes on beyond the inquisitive eye of the ego." For now, let's simply consider that when we say that thoughts create our reality, what we really are saying is that *consciousness* creates our reality—and that consciousness contains a part that is in our awareness and a part that is subjective to our awareness. It is the combination of both aspects of our consciousness that creates our reality. Interestingly, the mystic Ernest Holmes (who frequently taught that thoughts are things) defines *thought* as "the movement of consciousness." A closer reading of Holmes shows that he did not intend for us to have such a limited concept of the word *thought* so as to interpret it to mean only conscious thought.

Let's get back to using the Law of Attraction. Imagine that you have three buckets of thoughts, into which you put your mental energy. These three buckets can be seen as a continuum. At one end of the continuum are thoughts regarding what we observe in our life but don't want. Next are thoughts related to the aspects of our lives that we appreciate. Finally, up the continuum are thoughts that relate to manifestations that are not currently in our lives but that we desire. Our goal in using the Law of Attraction is to move our thoughts up that continuum.

Frequently, we look at life and see things "out there" in the physical world that are less than what we desire. So, what are our emotions and beliefs regarding these events in our lives? If our emotions and beliefs are along the lines of, "Woe is me!" or something similar (I'll never do that, I've always been fat, I'll never be rich, etcetera), then we tend to direct our mental energy in using the Law of

Attraction into receiving more of the same. However, if we can view events we don't desire as being useful for helping us recognize what we don't want in life, then we give them less energy and they tend to dissipate. This "turning from conditions" towards higher possibilities is probably the hardest thing to do in using the Law of Attraction.

One of the best tools for moving our thoughts and emotions away from the apparent limitations of the physical life we perceive is to focus on things for which we feel appreciation. The more we can shift our thoughts into that bucket (where we are appreciative for that which we have right now), the less energy we are putting in the first bucket. And, in that process, the more we are moving up the continuum. Having gratitude for the challenges in our lives and the lessons they teach us is a great way to move from bucket one to bucket two. I encourage you to look around at your life, at everything large and small for which you are happy, and feel appreciation for it. For example, this morning I was appreciative of my hot coffee, my warm house, my clothes, my friends, my wife, my family, my dog, and even the railing I was holding onto as I walked up the stairs. Do you get the picture?

The process of feeling appreciative for everything in your life makes it easier to move your thoughts to the third bucket. Here you visualize your life as it can be. You see in your mind that which may not be in physical form yet, but you know that it's coming. You release attachment to how it might show up, and just know that it will. You combine your thoughts with your emotions. That is, you couple your "conscious" thoughts with your "subconscious or subjective" thoughts, which give rise to your emotions.

In a sense, you have all parts of your thoughts (or consciousness) in alignment, knowing that this positive future is out-picturing in your life now. Then you simply allow the Law of Attraction to work.

Finally, the third reason people often experience some apparent proof that the Law of Attraction doesn't work relates to their not understanding that the manifestations of "creative mind" are not controlled by only their "personal use of mind." This is one of the biggest misconceptions regarding the Law of Attraction and the power of our thoughts.

Those who confuse this point frequently offer this thought experiment: If one person is thinking one thing and another person is thinking another, and the two thoughts are in conflict, whose thought wins? Here's a good example: Two drivers are approaching the same intersection from different directions on a collision course, and both are affirming that the light will be green for them when they reach the intersection. Who gets the green light?

When such a question is posed, the person asking it has an underlying assumption that there are two different minds thinking opposing thoughts, so there is conflict. What is not considered is that in reality, there is only one mind with two individual expressions using it. The two drivers are aware only of their individual thoughts. At the level of "big mind," there is greater awareness and a higher intention. At the individual level, it appears that one person "won" and one person "lost"—one person got a green light, the other red. At the higher collective consciousness level, we see there are no winners or losers. At this higher level, there is an outcome that is in alignment with a greater need that transcends the individual minds' desires. It is that greater collective consciousness intention that serves the greater needs of all—that collapsed the infinite possibilities down into the manifest experience. In some cases, the greater need may be served by giving one of the drivers a green light. In other cases, the greater need may be served by allowing the lights to operate on their programmed sequence. There may even be some other reason "driving" the outcome. No matter what manifests in such situations, we have to assume that the intentions of higher mind were served. Those who have trouble accepting the Law of Attraction will see this as some kind of copout. Those who can shift their perception from seeing individuals having their "own minds" to realizing that individuals are all ultimately "using one mind" will know this to be true.

There is another way of considering that it is not simply "our personal use of mind" that is in play in the act of creation in our world in a particular moment. In this broader perspective, we must acknowledge that "Big Mind" has already been setting things in motion before this instant. The wheels of manifestation were already set in motion for this moment, by prior acts of thinking. Things that are occurring around me are the result of prior thinking either by me, others, or the general tendency of our collective consciousness. But that doesn't call for me to have a defeatist attitude and think I cannot impact things. No, it is more important for me to consider that in a particular moment there are two aspects of thought that can create: prior thoughts that may still be creating the experience, and my introduction of a new thought into the mix, which may change the current moment or a future one.

Finally, for those readers who may still be having some internal refusal to believe that our thoughts have creative power, consider this: To benefit from the rest of the information in this book, you don't have to "believe in the Law of Attraction." What I would ask that you at least acknowledge that thoughts can lead to action. If you think about raising your right arm, you will raise your right arm. You can consciously choose whether to continue reading this book or not. Most (if not all) of your successes in life began with you thinking about them. Most business leaders recognize the power of crafting a powerful vision and mission statement to drive their endeavors. These are simply thoughts written down, so others can consider them.

I will remind you that anything you put into practice in your life begins with a thought. In the next chapter, we will consider how an invisible package of beliefs called a *worldview* can quietly guide what thoughts you have.

Chapter Four

The Evolution of Our Worldviews

One of my goals in this book is to encourage your development of looking at life through an evolutionary lens. So far we've laid out a theory of our spiritual evolutionary path as offered by various mystics and writers. We also have looked at Big History—academia's attempt to summarize scientific findings into a modern creation story, a story that is also about our evolution. And we have considered the unique status of consciousness as a major player in this evolutionary narrative. Hopefully, that "lens" is starting to take shape.

Although the rise of self-aware consciousness, coupled with the ability to learn and pass along that learning to others, was seen as a major line of demarcation between the status of "pre-humans" and our current status as "human being" (Homo sapiens sapiens), we have no definite point in time when we know this transition was made. Current scientific guesses are around 200,000 years ago.

What was consciousness like for these early humans? Was it, in essence, similar to our current experience? Was our internal experience of red flowers the same then as it is now? Or has it evolved in some way, such that the qualities of our experiences have changed? These are questions for which we may never have complete answers. However, there is some evidence regarding how our consciousness may change based upon the impact of external forces.

Just as our physical bodies evolved over millions of years to adapt to best fit their environment, so has our consciousness shifted in reaction to our external situations. Obvious examples of human adaptations in conscious awareness come from the work of anthropologists. (For instance, humans living in the Amazon jungle have developed skill different from those of Eskimos living in the Arctic). In each case, humans were able to adapt special skills and perceptions to best fit the environment in which they were living. But are such examples actually evidence of evolution of consciousness, or simply evidence of the flexibility of our consciousness to adapt "on the fly" to current life circumstances?

Another example of our consciousness shifting in response to our external world relates to the concept of *worldviews*. My first exposure to the idea of worldviews came a number of years ago when I first heard about the work of Clare Graves and Spiral Dynamics. This theory helped me to begin understanding why the religious and spiritual beliefs of so many people differed and why I resonated with the teachings of Ernest Holmes.

One of the first things that attracted me to the work of Ernest Holmes and the Science of Mind was its view of God. The idea that God is a power that moves in and through everything, as that thing, totally resonated with me. Although at an early age I was trained to think of God as "an old man in the sky", I had grown beyond that concept.

In addition to its view of the Divine or God, I also loved that Ernest Holmes' philosophy blessed all paths to God, recognizing how they serve the whole of life. Yet, this opinion or belief is not shared by many "mainstream" religions. I often think that if everyone studied and applied the concepts of Science of Mind, we would bridge the differences of separation that appear to exist in the outer world.

But then, I wonder about questions such as: Why do people think so differently? Why is there so much conflict in the world among religions, and between the belief systems of spirituality and science? Why is it that people cannot see beyond their differences to embrace their common unity? Why do people have such drastically different visions of God? In Spiral Dynamics, I found a theory that helps me answer those questions.

Spiral Dynamics is a scientific theory derived from the work of Clare Graves, PhD, in the early 1970s, and popularized since 1996 by Don Beck, Chris Cowan, and others. It describes a process by which humanity develops and moves through an upward spiral of emerging values (or ways of looking at the world) that arise in response to our changing life conditions. Applying the model is useful for breaking down cultural barriers, assisting in organizational leadership, meeting varying educational needs, and more.

Understanding Spiral Dynamics allows me to enhance my use of Science of Mind principles. I know that how (and what) people think is what creates their lives. The better I understand why people think the way they do, the greater insight I have regarding underlying beliefs that may be limiting all of us. It also opens me to compassion and understanding when I am confronted with the limiting beliefs of myself and others. And most importantly, I recognize that Spiral Dynamics can help us bridge our differences in how we see God.

Ernest Holmes repeatedly stressed that we are evolving as a species, and he described where that evolution is taking us. He stated that, "Evolution is the emergence of that which already is in form, in an ever-upward spiraling" and "The whole process of evolution is to produce a being who can consciously co-operate with the Evolutionary Principle, which is Pure Spirit." Spiral Dynamics supports these ideas.

Just as Holmes developed the cross-disciplined philosophy of Science of Mind based on the golden thread of truth he saw among science, religion and philosophy; psychologist Graves first developed his theory of human development based on years of research into human values that crossed into the realms of psychology, sociology, and biology. His data indicated that human beings exist at different "levels of existence," where we exhibit behavior and values that are characteristic of people at that level. We learn our behavior and values in order to meet the needs of the life conditions that surround us. Yet, as we meet our needs at one level of existence, there emerges new life conditions which require us to grow. As Einstein said, "The significant problems we face cannot be solved at the same level of thinking we were at when we created them."

Spiral Dynamics maps a system of nine or more levels of consciousness or worldviews, through which humans move in order. For ease in describing the levels, they are color coded, although the colors assigned have no particular significance. These levels alternate between a focus on the external world and attempts to change it, and a focus on the inner world and attempts to make peace with it. When charted, this pattern of evolutionary consciousness resembles a spiral. New life conditions bring new levels of thinking, which bring new life conditions, in an ever-repeating pattern.

We do not all have the same life conditions; therefore we don't all have the same worldview. Ultimately, this is the crux of our differences. By looking at the differing levels of needs of individuals, groups, organizations, cultures, or countries, we can see that they often are operating with different views of what is important. Unfortunately, this usually is invisible to us. As Graves stated, the error most people make "is that they assume the nature of man is fixed and there is a single set of human values by which he should live."

Beck and Cowan suggested that these levels of existence are DNA-like codes called "value-memes" or "v-memes," which reside in the mind or brain. They stated that their potential is available to all of us, and that they are "awakened" as life conditions outside us interact with these latent systems within us. In Science of Mind terms, we might consider that these v-meme codes are a part of the One Mind, which is subjectively available to all of us. Holmes reminds us that, "This Mind contains everything that was ever thought or perceived. From it flow all ideas that are now inherent within it. Any demand made upon it creates a new idea." Hence, the demands of new life conditions bring forth from within our subjective minds the creation of the new, inherent worldview to deal with them. This is part of our evolutionary nature.

What are these Spiral Dynamics levels of existence, and how do they show our continued evolution? Let's look at them briefly.

First, early man was faced with life conditions of basic survival. This "beige" level of existence gave rise to a worldview related solely to meeting biological needs. We became aware that we were distinct selves, began to sense cause and effect in the outer world, and developed heightened sensory abilities to best survive in that world. As we began to meet these needs, we sensed a desire to foster group effort to support meeting our challenges. Hence, there arose the second (or "purple") level of existence, where we formed tribes to create safety and stability. Here, there emerged the belief in mystical spirits in nature, a seasonal sense of time, and the development of myth and tradition. However, as needs were met at this level, the security of the tribe was disrupted by the emergence of the personal ego and the sense that the self was more powerful than the tribe.

The third (or "red") level of existence brought forth our power impulses: the belief that "might is right"; a spontaneous, guilt-free, daring nature; the desire for immediate gratification, and a lack of concern for consequences. Historically, these were the powerful warlords creating a system of those in power and those who submitted to the powerful. Yet as our needs were met at this level, we began to reflect upon the unfairness of the system of haves and the have-nots. This gave search to our belief that there are forces guiding our destiny and a need to understand the underlying rules of life, giving rise to the fourth (or "blue") level of existence. Here we find a desire for meaning and purpose, a sacrifice now for rewards later, order and rules, and a need to control impulses, causing our newly found guilt. Historically, this level gave rise to our major religions and our systems of laws. However, as the needs of this level were met, we began to question the cost we paid in our loss of individual freedom due to absolutistic rules.

In the fifth (or "orange") level of existence, we began to question the rules, authority, and the delayed gratification of our needs. We began to strive to conquer the world, unlock its secrets, and achieve personal and material success. We sought pleasure in life *now*, not in the future. This level saw the rise of goal-oriented planning, economic competition, and the pursuit of scientific truths. But alas, our material success did not give us true happiness, and we began to turn inward to find our truth. The sixth (or "green") level of existence saw us begin to seek consensus for decisions, pursue humanitarian efforts, and display tolerance of personal differences. We sought harmony through belonging, acceptance, community, unity, and understanding our inner nature.

These six "first tier" levels are characterized by the fact that if you look at life through one of them, you don't recognize that there are other valid ways of looking at life. We can see this playing out in the world today as the various religious fundamentalists (blue) have conflict with one another over whose "truth," order, and God is the "right" one. We begin to understand why popular books written by scientists (orange) are driven to deny that God (or more accurately, the God as defined by the blue level) exists. We start to understand why well-intentioned humanitarian efforts (green) to improve the conditions in third-world countries often are exploited by the local leaders (red) who have not developed the conscience and rules that only come in the higher blue system.

Using the map offered by Spiral Dynamics, we can see why people often don't understand one another. We recognize why solutions developed at one level of thinking do not always work when imposed onto the life conditions of another level. And you can't just tell people to think differently, because their thinking generally is appropriate for them, given their experiences. As Don Beck asserts, "You can't say don't think that way, because they do think that way."

So, how do we begin to heal these differences? It is only with what Graves called the "momentous leap" into "second tier" consciousness where one begins to see the validity of these different worldviews. You come to understand not only that each person has the right to believe what they want, but that there is a good reason that they believe as they do. Their beliefs are serving to assist them with their current life conditions. To put this in Science of Mind terms, we begin to see perfection and wholeness in all of life as it plays out before us. Everything is in right and divine order, even if it is not what we may personally choose.

Ironically, Beck says this second tier emerges in response to the chaotic life conditions of a modern world where all these "competing" worldviews battle for control. With a higher awareness, we recognize that the solution to moving humanity up the evolutionary spiral is to help people meet the needs of their current life conditions. We can only do this with an awareness of where they are on the spiral of life. For them to meet their current needs allows the natural evolutionary process to bring the necessary emergence into their lives of the next level of the spiral.

Interestingly, it is in these second-tier levels of existence (yellow, turquoise, and the continuous development of still higher ones) that Spiral Dynamics' research finds human values emerging that are very much in alignment with the teachings of Science of Mind.

Spiral Dynamics shows that at these higher levels of consciousness, we begin to understand the big-picture view of living systems and the evolutionary flow of life, where chaos and change are a natural part of life. We begin to see the role that each of us plays in our own evolution.

At these higher levels, we honor and respect others' beliefs and worldviews, without necessarily agreeing with them. We acknowledge the connection between spirituality and physics. We focus on and see the good in all living entities. We expand our use of brain and mind tools for developing consciousness. We see the individual self as part of a larger, conscious, spiritual whole that also serves the self. And, we value the spiritual beliefs of all the other levels as we stand in awe of the overall cosmic order.

Spiral Dynamics shows us that as humans evolve, so does their view of the divine. The spirits that we saw in all of nature was a proper view for our purple mythic worldview. The "old man God in the sky" who judged us on our death met the needs of a blue worldview that desired a life of control and rules. Even the denial that God exists (which frequently comes with a fundamental scientific worldview) serves our needs at that level of understanding. God presents God to us in a manner that our level of consciousness can understand. This is part of the natural process. As Holmes says, "Evolution is the awakening of the soul to a recognition of its unity with the Whole." This is where both Science of Mind and Spiral Dynamics indicate that our consciousness is evolving.

Using Spiral Dynamics in connection with Science of Mind gives me hope. They both affirm that there is a natural direction in which our collective consciousness is ultimately evolving, and they affirm that we will ever be evolving. Holmes said, "What we must avoid, however, is the confusion which arises from a belief in final revelations, from the belief that all truth is at last discovered, or that some person or some system of thought has delivered the last word. There are no finalities in any science, any philosophy, or any religion. Through the continual emergence of the creative Principle, any last finality proves to be but the beginning of a new creative series. This eternal spiral, finding its base in the everlasting Reality, will never cease to emerge."

As I studied and implemented the ideas of Spiral Dynamics, I began visualizing an evolutionary spiral cycle of consciousness going back to those early humans who first crossed the threshold into self-awareness, and evolving upward to our current state of awareness. Looking back over the eons of human history, I realized that the part of our consciousness that forms this underlying worldview has shifted and evolved through these various stages in response to the conditions of human life. As our life conditions changed, so did our worldview of life. New worldviews "emerged" in response to these new conditions. Understanding the evolution of human worldviews helped me appreciate more deeply our evolutionary story.

Chapter Five

Crossing Our Next Threshold

As you begin to develop an evolutionary lens, you can't help but wonder what is next? Where is humanity going? Is there a direction to our evolution? As we mentioned in Chapter One, the answer you receive to the question of "What's next?" will depend upon who you ask.

Currently, most mainstream scientists live within the modern worldview—the orange meme in Spiral Dynamics. There have been great gifts given to humanity through the power of science. However, one of the vulnerabilities of scientific thinking is the devolution of thought into a dogmatic belief that everything is simply "matter" being acted upon by "laws," and that there is no purpose or direction behind life and the universe. Hence, many scientists discount the idea that there is any specific direction or "telos" to evolution. Obviously, I disagree.

There are a few evolutionary theorists and futurists who have pointed out where they think we are headed. We will consider some of their thoughts here. In addition, in my book, *Be Yourself: Evolving the World through Personal Empowerment*, I devoted a chapter to describing our potential future as seen by certain scientists, philosophers, and mystics. I will revisit that summary here later.

My main intention in this chapter is not to describe so much the ultimate endgame of human evolution as it is to discuss what I see as the characteristics of our next major threshold, one that is beyond the thresholds listed in our review of Big History.

In essence, I see this threshold as being one where we take charge of the influences on our lives of our animalistic past and begin to focus upon our spiritual future. While we live in the third dimension, we will always be influenced to a degree by our evolutionary past. This threshold, however, represents a major shift in human history where the majority of us are no longer controlled by physical needs, freeing us to direct our intentions towards living up to our highest potential. We move away from surviving and into thriving.

I like to visualize us as living with one foot planted in this third-dimensional world, where we have evolved physically through millions of years and are still influenced by the needs created through that past, and another foot planted in the spiritual world beyond this dimension, where we know greater possibilities exist. Let's explore this a bit.

Consider the work of Abraham Maslow and his hierarchy of needs. I've long been a student of Maslow's and devoted a number of pages to this motivational theory in my book, *Be Yourself*. Here's a quick refresher: Maslow studied high-achieving individuals to determine what motivated them. Over time, he realized that there was a hierarchical nature to what drives humans. Certain needs had to be met first, and it was only after fulfilling them that we could move up to "higher needs." As these new needs were met, we again moved up to new needs. If at any time any of the lower needs are not met, we revert back to attempting to have them met.

Eventually, Maslow charted this into a pyramid structure, with the lower needs on the bottom and the higher needs on the top. Our base needs were physiological (air, food, water, etcetera). Next were safety needs (security, employment, health, and so on). Next were love and belongingness needs (friendship, family, and sexual intimacy). Next were esteem needs (confidence, achievements, being respected by others, etcetera.. Late in his life, Maslow described the first four levels as being "deficiency needs." What he meant by this was that our lack or absence of something was what was driving us. We had a hole we needed to fill.

The highest level of Maslow's original pyramid was what he called *self-actualization needs*. Here we were called to express our creativity and problem-solving abilities and to become all that we could become in life. Later Maslow added another level he called *self-transcendence*. What he recognized was that at this highest level, we are motivated to transcend or move beyond our human experience. Maslow combined the levels of self-actualization and self-transcendence into what he called *being needs*. These were the highest reaches of human nature. Here we were not driven by lack, nor were we trying to fill a hole within us. Rather, Maslow felt that individuals motivated by *being needs* already felt they had everything they needed. Their lives were full, and they now were motivated to give to others out of that sense of fullness.

It's easy to see that the lower needs on Maslow's hierarchy relate to needs based on our animalistic past. It's also easy to see that the higher needs—the being needs, specifically—are driven by something from beyond this dimension. Maslow's hierarchy charts the development of our needs from animal to spiritual.

In Chapter Four, we reviewed the characteristics of each of the viewpoints described in the research of Clare Graves. Similarly, we can see that our early worldviews (whether from the distant past of humanity or the early years of our current offspring) are designed to meet life conditions based upon our animalistic past. And, as humanity developed toward higher worldviews, the highest outlooks on life were driven by more spiritual, holistic life conditions. Spiral Dynamics also points us to higher levels of consciousness, or what Graves called the "momentous leap" to second-tier consciousness. Again, it's easy to see a shift from our animal nature to our spiritual nature.

There are many forces at work that serve to keep us focused upon our base needs—our animalistic nature. In my opinion, the two biggest influences that hold us back are the messages we receive when we are young that were not "good enough," and the competitive nature of modern society, which frequently leads us to believe that our success is tied to the failure of others.

In his book, *A Hidden Wholeness*, Parker J. Palmer describes how we are born into a state of wholeness, but that we learn to hide our true identities from each other. In the process, we become separated not only from each other, but from our own souls. We end up living what he calls a "divided life." Somewhere within ourselves a still, small voice whispers our truth about ourselves and our work in the world. Yet, out of family and cultural training as well as fear of how we will be perceived, we don't listen to our truth. Instead, we live our lives outwardly as we think we are expected to live them.

This inauthenticity between how we live our lives and the truth we know about them comes with a steep price. We refuse to invest ourselves in our work, seeing our jobs as just a way to "make a living." We remain in situations and relationships that slowly kill our spirit. Ultimately, we begin to see ourselves as having two lives: the inner or backstage world of our truth that we hide from others, and our outward, onstage lives that we project to them.

Somehow, Palmer says, we must heal this divided life. When we fail to do so, our "inner light cannot illuminate the work we do in the world." Living behind an internal wall, we fail to let the light of the outer world into our inner darkness. Our relationships suffer, as those close to us sense the gap between our "onstage performance and backstage reality." Yet the movement to wholeness can be difficult to accomplish by ourselves. Palmer writes that "we need spaces within us and between us that welcome the wisdom of the soul." His belief is that somewhere within us is the wisdom we can tap that will bring us back to our state of wholeness.

In looking at my own life, as well as in working with others as a spiritual counselor, I can see the same pattern playing out over and over. We internalized at an early age that something was wrong with us, and that belief—frequently hidden from our consciousness—directs our actions so as to limit us from freely expressing ourselves. In the early pages of *Be Yourself*, I described the story of how my parents unintentionally negated my feelings over the loss of a nanny who had been my primary caretaker in the first two years of my life. Only years later did I discover that this event had been crucial in my forming a belief that somehow I was not as good as other people. Most psychological and spiritual counseling works with an individual's feelings of inadequacy or lack, feelings that often were created early in life.

Compounding the issue is that we live in a modern society that celebrates external success and invites comparisons between our lives and those being celebrated. We create a culture of celebrity that holds up the beautiful and the wealthy as the ideal. The more we hear it, the more we believe this is what we are supposed to aspire to. If we are not as wealthy or as beautiful as the role models, again, something must be wrong with us.

For us to move up from our animalistic past and towards our spiritual future, we need to let go of seeing ourselves as in a place of lack, not good enough, not worthy, and feeling shameful. We need to see our success as not based on any comparison with others, but rather be driven to live the highest possible life we can live. If there's any comparison to be made, it is not looking at our life against what others have or do, but looking at our life against what we know is possible for ourselves. Are we living up to our highest potential?

Developing an evolutionary lens that allows us to see that we were birthed from the same unity as every other person helps to eliminate the importance of comparing ourselves with them. They are simply having different experiences as their multiplicity within the unity. This new way of seeing life from an evolutionary standpoint allows us to take charge of our personal evolution. Our call is to answer what's next for us on our evolutionary journey—to look up the spiral of our life and see where we are called to express ourselves regardless of what others say or do.

As we move from being motivated by needs based on lack and towards *being needs*, although we let go of placing so much energy on the good opinions of others as to how we should live our lives, we don't totally divorce ourselves from the rest of humanity. As I wrote about extensively in *Be Yourself*, one of the essential aspects of living a spiritual life—a life motivated by self-actualization and self-transcendence—is that we are called to find our life purpose and to live it. In doing so, we also find that living a life on purpose becomes living a life of service to others and to the greater whole.

Hopefully you are beginning to see a pattern here—and a direction to our lives. Initially, we focus upon ourselves and our individual needs: healing our sense of lack and filling the holes we believe are within us. In time, as we move into wholeness in our individual lives, our attention turns outward, toward others, and we desire to be of service. As we move from selfishness to selflessness, from surviving to thriving, we also evolve into seeing that life is about more about cooperation than competition.

Cooperation is a vital ingredient in the next step on our path, according to evolutionary John Stewart, author of *Evolution's Arrow*. His book details the direction he believes evolution is taking us. From this, Stewart created what he calls his Evolutionary Manifesto, wherein he describes humanity's role in the future evolution of life. You can find his manifesto online at http://www.evolutionarymanifesto.com/.

His statement is a call for humanity to move into being more aware of the evolutionary process and to consciously direct it. He offers suggestions for how humanity can move forward on its evolutionary path and how moving in this direction can actually provide meaning to our lives.

To move forward, Stewart calls for us to transcend our past—meaning the hardwiring of biology (our animalistic past)—and to use the power of our consciousness via our intentions to move into the levels of cooperation needed to overcome our individual, selfish needs. As he points out, evolution up to this point in our history has used the competition created by external forces of survival to move us into internal cooperation. Cells banded together into larger and larger organisms, seeing that internal group cooperation had an evolutionary advantage. Humans banded together in tribes and cooperated to fend off the threat of other tribes, again offering an evolutionary survival advantage. The groups in which humans have cooperated have grown in size into countries or large multinational corporations, due to the competition with even larger external "others."

Stewart points out that to make the leap to cooperate with the entire family of humanity on planet Earth, we cannot rely on an external "other" threat (barring invasion by aliens). We are moving to a point where the only force we can use to overcome our selfish needs is an awareness of both the evolutionary process and our advantages in cooperation, even without an external threat. Of course, we could consider that the forces of the Earth as they react to the mistakes of humanity (global warming, oil spills, overpopulation, and so forth) may give us the competitive motivation to move into cooperation. However, some argue that the opposite effect might occur, reversing us into smaller groups as we break into greater competition to fight for limited resources. I hope they are wrong.

What Stewart sees as being essential is for us to let go of the limited notion that because we always have been driven by selfishness in the past, that precedent dictates our future. There is no "selfish gene," only selfish people— who can learn to cooperate with others even when it may not be in their personal self-interest. As Big History points out, what separates humans from what came before is our ability to learn, and to pass along that learning. Stewart believes that we can learn and teach others to be altruistic simply because we recognize it is the best way for us to further our positive evolution.

In *Be Yourself,* I provided a summary of where various scientists, philosophers, and mystics believed we were headed in our future. Here are the common positive themes I described:

- We live in peace.

- We all have access to economic and social advancement.

- We experience a melding of science and spirituality.

- We have the freedom to individually express our unique creative abilities.

- We live recognizing the interconnectedness of everything.

- We purposefully use the power of our consciousness.

- We meet our individual needs while meeting the needs of the greater whole.

- We recognize that we are evolving and consciously cooperate with the process.

- We recognize that we are on a spiritual path to be reunited with our source.

Such are the characteristics of the world I know we can —and will—create. These are the characteristics I believe will emerge as we move through this upcoming major human-spiritual threshold.

In summary, here are the aspects of this looming crossroads:

- We acknowledge and honor the blessings given us by our evolutionary past and our animal-based nature, yet we are no longer controlled by them.

- We recognize that we are moving up an evolutionary spiral in consciousness, where we are motivated by greater needs: self-actualization and self transcendence.

- We develop ways that allow every human to meet their basic needs (which come from our animalistic past) and to be offered the opportunity to focus upon our greater needs motivated by our spiritual future.

- We see the birth of each human as a gift to humanity, and are motivated to assist that child in meeting its needs and in knowing its wholeness from the beginning of its life.

- We recognize that although evolution has guided our past, we can now direct our evolutionary future.

In other words, we will learn to navigate the energetic tension between living in a world based upon our third-dimensional, animalistic past, and a world based upon the higher calling of our true spiritual nature. In navigating this dynamic space, we will live the highest possibilities for our life individually and seek to assist others in living theirs.

Chapter Six

The Evolution of Consciousness and God

Here we come to the consideration of whether or not our consciousness and God are evolving. If you accept that evolution is real—and I believe it is—hopefully by now you have developed a bit of that evolutionary lens. From this perspective, why wouldn't God be evolving?

Now let's stop and check in: Did you have a reaction to that question? Did something inside you say that can't quite be right? You might be thinking, "Well, maybe the answer to the question is God evolving is—it depends." Depends on what—how you define God? Let's consider that question.

First, if your worldview is one that includes what I called the old myth of God (the old man in the sky that is external to us), then you might be thinking, "How can this all-powerful Creator God be evolving? Would not this God be outside the physical realm of man and not be subject to the evolutionary forces we see at play?" That sounds logical to me.

Second, if your worldview is one that says there is no God and everything is simply part of the physical universe subject to physical laws, then you might be thinking, "The question is meaningless, as there is no God to evolve." That sounds logical to me.

Third, if your worldview is one that says there is a God but God is an infinite intelligence and energy that permeates everything, such that everything is in God but God is greater than everything, then you might be thinking, "God or Spirit has infused everything with its energy and intelligence as well as created such forces as evolution. Hence, Spirit is not evolving, but is experiencing the process of evolution through us." That sounds logical to me.

So then, is God evolving? The answer seems to be yes and no. Within an individual worldview, the God or non-God of that worldview is not evolving. But if we step back and look at the worldviews of humanity, then we can see that our concept of God is evolving in our consciousness.

Ernest Holmes wrote, "We can know no God external to that power of perception by which alone we are conscious of anything. God must be interpreted to humanity through humanity's own nature" and "God comes to us as we come to him / her." What he seems to be saying is that who or what God is to us depends upon our level of consciousness. God shows up to us in exactly the same way our own awareness defines how God should show up. Holmes is not alone in holding this viewpoint.

Robert Wright, in book, *The Evolution of God*, agrees, as he makes the following points: God doesn't evolve, we do. Our perception of God changes as our cultural needs change. We experience continuous positive change in the quality of our lives over time; therefore life has a "direction." And, "salvation" works to arrange the world so that its people find themselves and think of themselves more and more as interconnected, which is part of evolution's direction.

Ultimately, what I believe to be true is this: The ultimate source from which we sprang originally placed all of us here—all of us little pockets of consciousness—so God or Spirit could experience through us this third-dimensional life of separation and the experience of time. As we have moved through our evolutionary spiritual journey, we have certainly grown through stages of development regarding what our ultimate source is—that is, our view of God has evolved. And it will continue to evolve as our consciousness grows in our experience of the future. But as our ultimate source experiences this evolutionary process through us, does this source intelligence also somehow evolve based upon this new experience? Logic would say yes, but who am I to say?

One more thing to consider is that as our view of God evolves, so does our view on how we interact with God. Stated another way, our methods of prayer evolve to match our vision of God.

Let's quickly look at the evolutionary path of humanity using Spiral Dynamics memes as the underpinnings. When early humanity crossed the threshold in consciousness to the level of becoming self-aware, our ancestors lived off the land and sought basic survival (beige meme). In time they began to see the value in living together in clans (purple meme). At this level of consciousness, our ancestors were in tune with the passing of seasons and their interconnectedness to nature. Their view of God was one of magical powers rising out of a nature world. Their prayers came in the form of seasonal rituals, full of music, rhythm, and dance.

As humanity evolved, individuals developed strong

personal egos and sought power. This gave rise to the survival of the fittest, kings with their servants, tribal leaders with their followers, the haves and the have-nots (red meme). At this level of consciousness, our understanding of God grew out of "gods in nature" to the gods that were behind nature to a pantheon of gods ruled by one God (such as Zeus). Our new view of God brought a new way to honor him: temples and monuments, gifts and offerings, and sacrifices.

The sense of inequity at the tribal level led to a new level of consciousness where humanity sought order, structure, and rules. Here we sought meaning and purpose in living, and attributed a divine plan that was beyond our comprehension to explain life (blue meme). Our new view of God shifted from one powerful God who ruled other gods to simply being one God. This God communicated to us through tablets with rules, sacred texts with laws, and through others who claimed to be intermediaries. We prayed to this God through prayers of petition, asking for favors and intervention in our lives.

The Enlightenment brought the rise of science and rational thought. Humanity shifted its view of the world to sensing it as a machine that we could learn to control for our own benefit. Competition, technology, and material abundance (orange meme) brought with it a sense that the old man God in the sky was a myth we needed to release. The belief was that God is dead, and prayer is an outdated superstition.

Material wealth did not satisfy us, and we sought meaning in community and relationships. We began to explore consciousness itself, turning inward to find meaning. We believed that everyone was equal, and the Earth was here for all of us to share (green meme). We released dogma and sought to become spiritual but not religious. God was resurrected, but not as an external being. God became a "unity," a unified field of energy, an underlying intelligent force that pervaded everything. How do you communicate with an intelligent field of energy? You direct its flow as it moves through you. You see the power in your thoughts and consciousness, and consciously work to direct that power. As your development had just come through the level of science and reason, you attempt to apply logic to your prayers to convince yourself and shift your belief. Prayer is now an affirmative statement of truth placed into the infinite field of possibilities, collapsing the quantum uncertainties in the desired direction.

People new to New Thought teachings such as the Science of Mind generally resonate with applying logic and reason through a predefined five-step prayer process. Ernest Holmes called it "argumentative" prayer, as we argue with our own minds to convince it of the truth. The five steps take us from identification with the external world of matter to an inner world where we sense the interconnectedness of everything, the power embedded in it, and our ability to direct that power. Through connecting with Spirit, stating our truth, sensing gratitude, and releasing our awareness "into the flow," we convince our logical minds of the truth and power of our prayer. Our emotional certainty is seen as a critical factor in directing this flow.

What Holmes—and others—were teaching by way of this "evolved" type of prayer was that the true creative power was within us, and that we could employ it by moving our consciousness in the direction of that which we desired. In other words, he was tapping the creative ability of our own thoughts and calling us to use the Law of Attraction as our form of prayer.

By now you probably have considered where you are in this evolutionary process. In 21st-century America, most of us fall into one of three general categories, in our beliefs about God and prayer: (1) God is an external being to whom we pray; (2) God is a myth and prayer is superstition; or (3) God is an intelligent power that we can tap via our consciousness.

Again, Robert Wright made several key points that are worth listing: God doesn't evolve, we do. Our perception of God changes as our cultural needs change. There is a continuous direction toward positive change over time.

In fact, Wright sees this positive trend as potential evidence of a divine power when he says, "If history naturally pushes people toward moral improvement, toward moral truth, and their God, as they conceive their God, grows accordingly, becoming morally richer, then maybe this growth is evidence of some higher purpose, and maybe—conceivably—the source of that purpose is worthy of the name divinity."

Where, then, is this evolution taking us? How is our perception of God continuing to evolve? How is our method of communication with the divine growing? Both mystics and Spiral Dynamics point in the same direction.

Joel Goldsmith, founder of the office of The Infinite Way, gave a lecture in 1959 in which he outlined this evolution of prayer we have been discussing. He said, "Most in orthodox religion still use pagan forms of prayer, which came to them when their churches were first founded, and their own forms of prayer had not developed: they used the prayer of petition... these ancient paganistic forms of prayer were the only forms of prayer the church had to work with... There is nothing wrong with these forms of prayer, any more than there is anything wrong with our form of treatment... It isn't a question of right or wrong; it is a question of the degree of consciousness. Because we are in a human state of consciousness at the moment, it is necessary that we start our prayer work with words and thoughts. In the metaphysical world these are called treatments; in the mystical world they're called realizations. The attainment of harmony is never accomplished by words or thoughts... They are but the introductions, the aids, given to bring us into an atmosphere where words and thoughts are no longer necessary to lift us to an inner communion through which God's grace reaches us."

Ernest Holmes also spoke of this evolutionary process. He advised us that "God comes to us as we come to him" meaning that how we see God and communicate with God depends upon our consciousness. "God is not a becoming God. God is not an evolving God. God is that which was, is, and will remain perfect, complete, happy, and harmonious." Again, God is not evolving—humanity and its perception of God are evolving.

Although Holmes taught the argumentative style of prayer described above, which was designed to shift our consciousness (a method to meet us where we were in our awareness: desiring logic and reason and needing to "convince ourselves" of the prayer's truth), he also taught a method called *realization*. In this method, one did not need convincing; one went straight to the truth. He defined *realization* as turning to that Living Presence within and recognizing It as the One and Only Power in the Universe, and unifying with it. He stated, "There is a point in the supreme moment of realization, where the individual merges with the Universe, but not to the loss of his individuality; where a sense of the Oneness of all Life so enters their being that there is no sense of otherness."

Spiral Dynamics tells us that humanity is making a great leap in consciousness. As we step into the second tier of awareness, we are able to see the entire spiral below us and value each level and stage as being necessary for our perfect unfoldment. We see the interconnectedness of all of nature; we understand its natural systems and flows (yellow and turquoise memes). We begin to see our individual self as part of a greater Self—the conscious, spiritual whole, where everything is part of one great living system... where we value all religions and all spiritual paths, seeing their necessity to bringing us to this point on our journey... where we live with wonder, awe, unity, harmony, and love.

My wish is that as you've read this, you have stepped outside our evolutionary path for a moment in your awareness and witnessed it from a higher level, where you can see its beauty and perfection and view where you are along the road. Hopefully you have glimpsed both the path you have walked spiritually and the road that lies ahead. Evolution's arrow is returning us all back home. Our consciousness is evolving back to unity with the divine. Your next step calls you. As you surrender to the next steps in your evolution, the question is, how can you positively direct your evolution?

Chapter Seven

Our Personal Conscious Evolution

My intention for you is that in reading this brief book, you have been able to develop a sense of the evolutionary lens I mentioned. And I hope you feel called to make some changes in how you live your life, based on this new outlook.

But what can you do? How does knowing that we are on this spiritual evolutionary journey translate into any actionable item?

Ultimately, identifying the appropriate action needs to come from within yourself. Each of us has the choice of whether to cooperate with this evolutionary process or not. If you wish to facilitate your personal evolution (which of course facilitates our collective evolution), here are seven key actions that will move you in a positive direction. All these steps are important. The first ones lead you to go within; the later ones move you out into the world.

Turn inward. So much in our lives directs our senses outward that it's easy to live with the belief that all the stuff we sense "out there" is the only stuff that is real. A daily practice of turning inward allows us a degree of balance. It shows us a truer reality, where we know that there is a presence that connects all. It is important that our lives experience this base.

Set the vision. As we turn inward, it's important that we set a vision of where we see our lives headed. We must begin with the end in mind, and visualize the highest outcome for our lives. What is it we are called to be? This vision gives our life direction.

Feed the mind. We must continue to grow intellectually; we must continue to learn. It's too easy to stay in our comfort zone, only learning more about what we already know and only pursuing sources that are biased in the direction of our beliefs. We must continue to challenge ourselves by exploring new areas and new ways of looking at things.

Nurture the body. We must take care of the physical vehicles that serve us while we are on Earth. We must ensure that these "temples" are exercised and well fed.

Heal the shadow. We were born in wholeness, but most of us have forgotten that fact. We must recognize that our early life experiences have buried, deep within us, beliefs and motivations that must be healed. We must seek to understand why we believe or act as we do, when such beliefs or actions are not in the best interests of ourselves and others. We must seek out and employ established methods to bring our shadow into the light, so we can heal it and make a higher choice. Healing our shadow is an essential part of returning to the awareness that we are whole and complete.

Act in alignment. Our actions in the outer world must be in alignment with our vision for our life. Each of us has a unique creative ability we are called to express. As we express that ability in our work or play, we must consider how it serves our growth, both as individuals and as part of the collective humanity.

Cultivate relationships. As we move outward in our action in the world, we must seek to connect with others. Developing relationships heightens our sense of interconnectedness. Expanding our involvement with others allows our talents and gifts to touch them, and their gifts to touch us. The interplay of our individual evolutionary gifts expands their influence and speeds our collective growth.

These are the seven keys that I believe are essential for each of us to be utilizing in our personal growth. Each is important. If you need some ideas on creating specific activities within these areas of your life, I recommend the resources mentioned in the Annotated List of Resources, on integral life practice and the work of philosopher Ken Wilber.

Do these seven steps resonate with you? Are you developing all of them? How might you grow one that you are ignoring currently? Would you add any steps to this list?

Although you ultimately have to decide what action (if any) you will take based on how strongly the information in this book resonates as true for you, there are a number of likely actions that naturally flow from adopting a spiritual evolutionary viewpoint. Here are some areas for your consideration:

Have fun! It is a joyous gift to have the experience of living on Earth at this time! No matter what you are doing with your life, you should find that it is bringing joy and fun into your life. Life is too short, and goes by too fast to "sweat the small stuff." Let go of petty concerns and small worries, let things slide off of you, and don't hang on to feelings of being "wronged." All of this tends to distance you from the sense of joy. Affirm and know each day that you are going to enjoy that day—and then do so! Make it a point to bring fun into your life and to everyone around you.

Develop an Evolutionary Outlook on Life. Often we become so mired in the daily events of our lives that we forget the larger story playing out all around us. If we can step back and take a moment each day to contemplate the bigger picture, we can begin to appreciate at a deeper level our spiritual evolutionary journey. Reflecting on both the "big history" of humanity's journey through time and your own personal developmental story allows you to see that there is a growth-oriented trajectory to both. It benefits us to realize that the challenges faced by humanity collectively, or by you individually in the past, were experiences necessary to facilitate growth. Realizing that fact allows you to eliminate (or at least reduce) your concerns about current global or personal tests. This evolutionary outlook also calls your attention toward the future and allows you to consider how you can assist in achieving our highest outcome.

Being Kind to Yourself. It is highly likely that you have been taught that you were not good enough, or were unworthy on some level. Your parents or caretakers most likely did not purposely instill your sense of a lack of self-worth. Yet, if at any of level of your consciousness there is a belief that you don't deserve all the goodness of life, then you need to change that thought. You are worthy. You deserve love and kindness. Give yourself permission to treat yourself with kindness. Forgive yourself for past mistakes and move on.

Let Go of Your Concern About What Others Think of You. This is a major concern for many people. First, if you have self-worth issues (as mentioned in the previous item), you may already have difficulty not comparing yourself to others and seeing yourself as lacking. But even beyond that, so many of us want to "fit in." Consider Maslow's Hierarchy of Needs, and Maslow's assertion that one of our basic "deficiency needs" was trying to fill a hole within us that wanted love and belongingness. We face this interesting tension, where we want to express ourselves in our own unique way, yet hold ourselves back out of concern for what others will think. The truth is that cultural norms will always resemble a bell-shaped curve. The vast majority of people will orient themselves towards the middle, so as to be like everyone else. But then there'll always be outliers at the edges—people less concerned about fitting in with the masses. It's at the edges that humanity has always grown and evolved. One visual image I like is putting a bell-shaped curve on a timeline, where the past is on the left and the future is on the right. The outlying people on the right are the futuristic thinkers that are assisting humanity in its evolution. They are dragging the whole bell curve to the right. On the far left hand are the people who are so mired in tradition and the past that they are, with every inch of their being, fighting moving forward. Then there are most people, midway between living in the past and moving towards the future. To be an evolutionary force, you need to be living out on the right-hand side—the "growing edge," where you are pushing your life forward without concern for the good opinions of others.

Being Kind to Others. Similarly, other people you encounter will have most likely developed their own sense of feeling unworthy. This can show up in relationships in many ways, including many that push your buttons. As you interact with others, always remember the Golden Rule and treat them as you would like to be treated. Treat them kindly, even when they don't treat you that way. Maintain healthy and appropriate boundaries, but always try to do no harm.

Meditation and Spiritual Practice. The outer world is continuously feeding us information that we are separate individuals in competition with one another. We need to develop experiences that remind us of the opposite. Taking time each day for some spiritual practice that develops a sense of unity is an important part of the evolutionary path.

Begin to Cultivate an Awareness of the Power of Your Thoughts. Whether you believe in the Law of Attraction are not, the fact is that what we focus our thoughts upon is what we tend to grow in our lives. What do you want to grow? Make a written list and review it daily. Consider imagining that everything on your list is already in your life. Practice this over and over each day. Then be open to taking any appropriate action, as opportunities arise that would bring more of the things on your list into your life.

Develop a Sense of Appreciation for Life. This is a great gift we have been given. No matter what your life experiences have been, ultimately our time here on Earth must be seen as good. Consider those things for which you are grateful, and keep a gratitude journal. Focus your energy and attention on the areas where the goodness lies in your life, and that goodness will expand.

After Your Basic Needs Are Met, Help Others Meet Theirs. You can't thrive if you're in survival mode, and neither can anyone else. It's essential that you take care of yourself, but at a certain point it's also essential that you let go of the need to continuously accumulate more, while others around you are still in survival mode. How you help others is up to you. The three general ways that we can give are through our "time, talent, and treasures." *Time* means volunteering to serve, such as tutoring kids or serving in a soup kitchen. *Talent* means using our special abilities to assist others, such as teaching or building houses or writing books. And *treasure* means giving of our money or our material possessions, such as donations to charity.

Find Your Purpose in Life and Begin Living It. At some level, each of us is aware that we are here on planet Earth for some specific purpose. Frequently, we ignore life's messages about that purpose, thinking that it's unrealistic. It's time to pay attention to those messages, identify that inner calling, and find a way to begin acting upon it. My book, *Be Yourself: Evolving the World through Personal Empowerment,* was all about techniques to help you find your purpose. When you begin living on purpose, your life will unfold in magical ways, and your happiness will expand. If it's what you came here to do, then why aren't you doing it?

Help Others Find Their Purpose in Life. If you have a purpose, then others have a purpose too! If your life will expand in great and wonderful ways by you living on purpose, then the lives of others can expand in the same way if they live on purpose. As your life grows by living on purpose—and with the expanded awareness that we are all connected and are moving through the same evolutionary journey—then one of the most important things you can do with your life is to help every person you meet to identify their purpose and begin living it.

Be of Service to the World. We are all connected, we are all one, we are all on the same journey. The more you embody that truth, the more you are called to be of service. When I give to you, I am giving to everyone and everything—including myself. When I am living on purpose and have a sense of our unity, my purpose becomes to serve in my own unique way.

Be Love, Give Love, Receive Love. Love is an evolutionary force. When I experience love, it draws me out of my sense of separation and enhances my sense of connectedness to others. When others experience love, it does the same for them. The more we foster love in our personal sphere of influence, the greater we are moving humanity along its evolutionary path. How do we foster love? We do this simply by being a loving individual. We give love freely to all, recognizing and knowing at the deepest levels of our being that every person we meet is connected to us at some level and is deserving of our love. As we love that person, we are loving everyone, including ourselves. As others wish to bestow love upon us, we should be open to receiving it. We should recognize that love is an energetic flow, and never let that flow stagnate or stop. We must always be a conduit for maintaining the flow of love. *Be love* every day.

Each of us has a choice.

On the one hand, we can live in fear and separation. We can live in survival mode. We can believe that life is about competition and survival of the fittest. We can believe that there are limited resources, and that if we are not careful, we won't get our fair share. We can dislike others who are different from us. We can buy into our limiting beliefs and feel unworthy and shameful. We can ignore our calling and spend our time doing something else, even though we're unhappy.

On the other hand, we can live in love and unity. We can thrive. We can recognize that life is about cooperation and caring for one another. We can believe that there is enough for everyone if we share. We can seek to understand those who appear different from us, and then learn and grow through the experience. We can heal past hurts and let go of false beliefs. We can answer our calling and spend our time here in the third dimension immersed in the bliss of happiness and joy.

What are you going to choose?

We are at an interesting place in human evolution. I am asking you to consider moving forward in your life toward your highest possibilities. The more of us who move forward into that growing edge, the more our collective consciousness will assist in bringing all of humanity to its highest potential.

I hope you realize by now that transcending the third dimension doesn't mean that you don't care about life right now, here on Earth. It isn't about floating off the planet in a state of blissful oblivion. It isn't about walking away from your personal responsibilities.

Instead, to transcend the third dimension is to let go of the belief that this physical life and your individual success while living it is tied to holding certain religious beliefs, gathering the most material wealth, or winning in some competition with other humans. To transcend the third dimension is also to let go of seeing your life as somehow lacking in such a way that you are focused on filling that lack based on things in the external world (money, power, relationships, love, sex, and so forth). To transcend the third dimension is to let go of your attachments to all the stuff "out there."

But transcending the third dimension is not just about "letting go"—it's also about claiming certain things. When you transcend the third dimension, you recognize that coming here into this experience was truly a glorious gift to your soul. You recognize that you were already whole and complete when you came here, so there is nothing out there that you truly "need" to be whole. This shift in perception allows you to enjoy, at a deeper level, every moment of your life—every relationship, every experience. In this new perspective, you recognize that you are "in this world, but not of this world." We understand what Teilhard de Chardin meant when he said, "We are not human beings having a spiritual experience. We are spiritual beings having a human experience." We recognize that we are living in two worlds simultaneously. And that realization allows us to transcend the limits created by the thought that we were only human animals living in third-dimensional space and fourth-dimensional time.

It is time to transcend the third dimension.

A higher and greater life awaits you!

Annotated List of Resources

Conscious Evolution

If you have started developing an "evolutionary lens" and want to read more about our spiritual evolutionary journey, here are some recommended resources:

Gilbert, Mark. *Be Yourself: Evolving the World Through Personal Empowerment*, Conscious Bridge Publishing, 2012. This book is about our evolutionary journey and how we are at a crossroads in that journey. Ultimately, we hold the keys to our highest future. The three keys the book offers to this future are to focus on how we are alike rather than how we are different, to keep our thoughts and attention directed toward a positive vision for that future, and to listen to our inner calling to follow it by living a life of passion and service. The book includes numerous exercises to identify your calling. In addition, my current writings on this topic can be found at www.consciousbridge.com.

Dowd, Michael. *Thank God for Evolution*, Council Oak Books, 2007. Dowd was a fundamentalist Christian minister who evolved into a greater appreciation for evolution, which expanded his spiritual outlook. He and his wife, Connie Barlow, travel the country teaching about our evolutionary journey. This book is essential reading for those interested in the topic, as it does an excellent job of melding our biological understanding of evolution with the new spiritual story it supports.

Hubbard, Barbara Marx. *Conscious Evolution*, New World Library, 1998. Hubbard's material was some of the first that called for us to develop a new story of creation and recognize our role in the next great awakening, and I highly recommend it. Also check out her website for the Foundation for Conscious Living at www.barbaramarxhubbard.com. The site includes information on her DVDs, *Humanity Ascending* and *Visions of a Universal Humanity*, which are excellent resources.

Swimme, Brian and Berry, Thomas. *The Universe's Story: From the Primordial Flaring Forth to the Ecozoic Era*, Harper Books, 1992. This was one of the first books calling for us look for meaning in our lives, within the story of science and the Big Bang. More recently, Swimme produced a short movie titled *Journey of the Universe* (it has a companion book), which also help to visualize this evolutionary story. Information is available at www.journeyoftheuniverse.org.

Big History

One of the best resources is the course *Big History* from The Great Courses with Professor David Christian. This lecture-style program is available in audio or video. All their classes are available at www.thegreatcourses.com. You also can find a very good (and brief) TED talk by Christian at www.ted.com/talks/david_christian_big_history.html. Bill Gates is funding a project to make Big History available to high schools through the Big History Project; information is available at www.bighistoryproject.com. Recently the History Channel produced a 10-part video series on Big History; information is available at www.history.com/shows/big-history.

Consciousness

If you are interested in reading about the study and research of consciousness, there is so much content available on the topic that it can be overwhelming. One thing that is essential in reading about consciousness is to ascertain the worldview of the author so you will understand the assumptions behind their content. Most material in the mainstream comes from the "brain = mind" materialist viewpoint. However, I recommend the following two books:

Ornstein, Robert. *The Evolution of Consciousness: the Origins of the Way We Think*, Simon & Schuster, 1991. Ornstein is a psychologist who writes extensively about consciousness and the brain. This book is a good introduction to a materialist viewpoint on how consciousness developed though physical evolution—but Ornstein is, in my opinion, open to other possibilities regarding the topic. More recently, he has been working on a website to document the story of the human journey of consciousness (see www. humanjourney.us).

De Quincey, Christian. *Consciousness from Zombies to Angels: The Shadow and the Light of Knowing Who You Are*, Park Street Press, 2009. I highly recommend this book as an alternative to the strictly materialistic viewpoint. De Quincey also teaches and coaches on the subject of consciousness. More information on his work can be found at www.christiandequincey.com.

Worldviews

There are two primary sources of material that I recommend to learn more about worldviews: material on Spiral Dynamics, and basic introductory material on Integral Theory.

For information on Spiral Dynamics:

Beck, Don and Cowan, Chris. *Spiral Dynamics*, Blackwell Publishing, 1996. This is the basic "bible" on the subject, although it is not the most accessible resource for a new student. The best introduction is an audio presentation from Sounds True titled "Spiral Dynamics Integral." Here is a link to that company's website for information: www.soundstrue.com. Alternatively, there is very good introductory material on the internet that can be found by searching on the term "spiral dynamics."

For an introduction to Integral Theory:

Wilber, Ken. *The Integral Vision: A Very Short Introduction to the Revolutionary Integral Approach to Life, God, the Universe, and Everything,* Shambhala, 2007. This short book is absolutely the best resource to date on understanding integral theory. However, I have to add that Integral Theory is more than just worldviews. Wilber attempts to tie all truths into one framework he calls his AQAL model (meaning "all quadrants, all lines, all levels, all states, all types"). It is not as daunting to grasp as many people claim. I also have a brief introduction to Integral Theory on www.consciousbridge.com. To move beyond this book, consider the next one.

Wilber, Ken. *A Brief History of Everything*, Shambhala, 2001. This book is written as a dialogue, and the style makes Wilber's philosophy come alive. His thinking has continued to grow beyond this book, but the material here is very accessible. Sounds True also offers several audios of Wilber's work; I recommend *Kosmic Consciousness*. In addition, you can find great introductory information on the internet at www.integrallife.com. There are many other sources of information on this topic on the internet as well.

Evolution's Direction

I am listing the work of Abraham Maslow in this section, but it could just as well have been included under other topic headings. I see Maslow as important for our evolution because he studied "high performers." He was looking at the highest reaches of what was possible for humans; hence he was really looking at our ultimate direction, if we live up to our potential. Here are some Maslow resources I have found helpful.

Maslow, Abraham. *The Farther Reaches of Human Nature*, Penguin / Arkana, 1993. This book is a collection of essays written by Maslow and collected and published posthumously. It represents his thinking on the topic at the end of his life, and reflects how he had evolved in his viewpoints on motivation and his hierarchy. While not an easy read, it is worthwhile.

Maslow, Abraham. "A Theory of Human Motivation," *Psychological Review*, 1943. This is the basic outline of the famous Hierarchy of Needs. (The pyramid picture of it was added later.) You can find this on the internet by searching on the title.

Does evolution have a direction? It depends on whom you ask. I think it does, and I wrote about it in my book, *Be Yourself*. One of the major influences of my thinking on this topic is the work of John Stewart:

Stewart, John. *Evolution's Arrow,* Chapman Press, 2000. Stewart has made his book and summary "manifesto" available for free on the internet. Go to this website, http://users.tpg.com.au/users/jes999/, or search on "Evolution's Arrow" to find it. You also can find a Kindle version of both *Evolution's Arrow* and his manifesto, with additional content, available at a low cost on Amazon.com. I highly recommend it.

Spiritual Evolution

There has been a blossoming of this topic in recent years, and I suggest you can type the phrase into your search engine to find a plethora of available information. You will, of course, find a wide range of views and a broad array of material. I specifically recommend (in addition to my other books and website) the recent book by Carter Phipps, *Evolutionaries: Unlocking the Spiritual and Cultural Potential of Science's Greatest Idea*. Note that this topic is so broad that the resources on Integral Theory, Spiral Dynamics, and others listed here also touch on the subject.

I obviously wrote this book with a bias toward the Science of Mind and Spirit. There are many resources available on this topic. Keep in mind that Science of Mind is about much more than our evolution; it is about how to live our lives more spiritually and abundantly. Here is the Science of Mind "bible":

Holmes, Ernest. *The Science of Mind*, Tarcher Penguin Books, 1938. I must warn the beginning reader that this can be a tough read, but it is worth the effort. Holmes's use of words can be a bit archaic, and sometimes the meanings can be different than the way we understand the terms. Fortunately, there is a glossary in the back of the book. Holmes also wrote many other books on the subject. Some of them, such as *The Basic Ideas of Science of Mind*, may provide a better introduction. Those that are interested can also find introductory classes at any member community of Centers for Spiritual Living (for information, go to www. csl.org).

In the text, I referenced the work of Robert Wright:

Wright, Robert. *The Evolution of God*, Back Bay Books, 2010. This is an interesting book that provides an historian's take on the topic of the evolution of God, prayer, and related topics.

Directing Our Own Evolution

This is another topic for which you could use the other resources (especially Barbara Marx Hubbard) as a basis for understanding how you can consciously direct your individual and our collective evolution. However, I will highlight a few things that are directed specifically at the "personal action" aspect of the subject:

First are my own books. The concept of developing an

evolutionary lens, and then applying it, is the underpinning of all of my writing. My first book, *Be Yourself: Evolving the World Through Personal Empowerment,* and my website, www.consciousbridge.com, address this topic. In addition, two recent books of mine are directly focused on the "action" side of the equation:

Gilbert, Mark. *Our Spiritual Rights and Responsibilities,* Conscious Bridge Publishing. 2014. This book outlines, from an evolutionary perspective, the key rights we have by virtue of being born as humans having this spiritual experience. But with rights come responsibilities. Ultimately, the book calls us to live our fullest life as a part of our rights, but to make sure that in doing so, we do no harm to others—and do what we can to help other live their highest potential.

Gilbert, Mark. *Becoming a Spiritual Change Agent,* Conscious Bridge Publishing, 2014. A series of essays themed towards how we can live the highest possibilities for our lives, serve as change agents in the world, and ultimately be a "bridge" between our current world and the highest future we know is possible.

Finally, although the work of Ken Wilber was mentioned above, I also want to provide one resource of his that is very "action-oriented":

Wilber, Ken; Patten, Terry; and Leonard, Adam. *Integral Life Practice: a 21ˢᵗ Century Blueprint for Physical Health, Emotional Balance, Mental Clarity, and Spiritual Awakening,* Integral Books, 2008. This book takes the Integral Theory's "AQAL" way of looking at life and applies it to the world of personal practices. You can "chunk up" your life into modules and then have developmental practices that help your personal growth in those areas of your life. The book contains many good ideas for things you can do to help you grow.

About the Author

Mark Gilbert is a spiritual teacher and writer who lives in Colorado with his wife, Mary, and his chocolate Lab, Harmony. He is the author of the books, *Be Yourself: Evolving the World Through Personal Empowerment, Our Spiritual Rights and Responsibilities*, and *Becoming a Spiritual Change Agent*. Mark also publishes the blog site, *Conscious Bridge* (consciousbridge.com). He holds a Bachelor of Science degree in Psychology from the University of Alabama, Birmingham, and a Master's degree in Consciousness Studies from the Holmes Institute. In addition, he supports the growth of spiritual centers around the globe in his role with the international headquarters of the Centers for Spiritual Living in Golden, Colorado. Mark is a certified trainer in Spiral Dynamics and frequently writes for *Science of Mind* magazine.

CPSIA information can be obtained
at www.ICGtesting.com
Printed in the USA
FSHW012311010119
54770FS